SHIFT IN INDIAN POLITICS

SHIFT IN INDIAN POLITICS

1983 Elections in Andhra Pradesh and Karnataka

Edited by

GEORGE MATHEW

Christian Institute for the Study of Religion and Society
Bangalore New Delhi

CONCEPT PUBLISHING COMPANY
NEW DELHI

First Published 1984

Published by
Naurang Rai
Concept Publishing Company
H-13 Bali Nagar
NEW DELHI-110015 (India)

Printed by
Asia Composer
at Sunil Printers, Naraina
NEW DELHI-110028

Preface

The Christian Institute for the Study of Religion and Society (CISRS) and its founders who worked in different social concerns before the formation of the Institute in the forties and fifties were concerned with the growth of Indian democracy and social justice through the electoral process. This has resulted in a number of valuable studies on Indian democracy, political parties and social change since 1955.*

When Andhra Pradesh and Karnataka voted for a party other than the one they were voting since independence, the CISRS convened a writing party of distinguished scholars and political observers at the Institute for Social and Economic Change, Bangalore, to assess the importance of this for the political process and social change in India. Issues were analysed and drafts of some of the papers were discussed. The contributors to this volume, who are scholars in the respective areas of society and politics on which they have written, strongly argue that this election had significance for the future politics and centre-state relations in the country.

NEW DELHI

SARAL K. CHATTERJI
Director

February 1984

*See page 186.

List of Contributors

AMAL RAY

Professor of Development Politics and Administration and Head of Department, Administration Unit, Institute for Social and Economic Change, Bangalore. He is the author of *Federal Politics and Government* and co-author of *Political Development and Constitutional Change*.

BASHIRUDDIN AHMED

Director, Centre for the Study of Developing Societies, Delhi. He is the co-author of *Caste, Race and Politics: A Comparative Study of India and the United States* and *Citizens and Politics Mass Political Behaviour in India.*

LALITHA NATRAJ

Teaches in Institute of Development Studies, University of Mysore. Her special interests are political aspects of development and planning; state level politics in India. She contributes regularly to *Economic and Political Weekly.*

G. NARAYANA

Faculty member of the Administrative Staff College of India, Hyderabad. He has worked on several projects in the areas of political sociology, health and population programmes, and rural development; present areas of interest include bureaucracy and politics, health and population programme management.

V.K. NATRAJ

Reader in Institute of Development Studies, University of Mysore. His particular interests are decentralised planning, mobilisation of backward classes, and regional planning. Joint editor, *Regional Planning and National Development*, author *Decentralisation of Planning in India.*

K. RAGHAVENDRA RAO

Reader in the Department of Political Science at the Karnataka University, Dharwad. He writes poetry in English and translates Kannada poetry into English; currently working on a study of the theoretical encounter between Gandhi and Marx.

RATNA NAIDU

Faculty member (Sociology) of the University of Hyderabad, is the author of *Values in Models of Modernization* and *The Communal Edge to Plural Societies* and co-editor with P.C. Joshi *Studies in Asian Social Development.*

M. SHATRUGNA

Teaches physics in Gupta College, Hyderabad. A keen student of politics, he is a regular contributor to *Economic and Political Weekly* and *Mainstream.*

G. SRINIVAS

Research scholar in the Department of Sociology at the University of Hyderabad. He worked on "Congestion, ghetto culture and communal tension in the old city in Hyderabad" and continuing his study on "the impact of congestion on tensions" for Ph.D.

F.D. VAKIL

Reader in the Department of Political Science at the Osmania University, Hyderabad. Associated with several research projects on electoral politics and Indian political system, his specialization is electoral studies and rural politics.

Contents

List of Tables

1

INTRODUCTION

GEORGE MATHEW

ANDHRA PRADESH and Karnataka were two bastions of the Congress party. Even when many other states had rejected Congress rule[1], these two southern states stood by the oldest political party which had won independence for the country. Ironically, at a time when the Congress party at the centre was consolidating its power and a state like Kerala which had a tradition of non-Congress governments was limping back into its fold, the people of Andhra Pradesh and Karnataka were looking for alternatives which made them vote decisively for Telugu Desam Party (TDP) and Janata-Kannada Kranti Ranga respectively. This shift is of great significance for the polity in India.

Political analysts have offered several reasons for the voting behaviour of the two states comprising 51.2 million voters. Corruption in the ruling party, factionalism, erosion of the traditional support base of the Congress among the Scheduled Castes, Scheduled Tribes, minorities and other backward classes, poor performance of the party when in power and the resulting misery for the deprived sections of the society, Congress (I) central leadership's lack of respect for regional aspirations and the decline of prime minister Indira Gandhi's charisma—these are some of the reasons advanced to explain why the people opted for parties other than the one that had ruled for almost 35 years. Many of these aspects of the 1983 elections are discussed in their proper setting by the contributors to this volume.

Although the chapters were written by various authors, there is an underlying unity running through them. If people's will is allowed to have its way, (the fact of the matter is that in most countries of the world, people's will is not permitted to assert itself) in Indian polity unexpected changes do occur in the direction people have decided to take. There are several variables that have influenced this process in our country and will do so in future: and these are the focii of discussion in the book. K. Raghavendra Rao's approach is theoretical. He sees the Karnataka election as increase of "materialisation" of the people's culture and the growing shift from caste to class as the focus of identity. Lalitha Natraj and V.K. Natraj place the 1983 elections in the background of caste politics in Karnataka. They trace the development and the political role of backward classes and minorities from the first decade of this century up to the 1983 elections. The article points out that Devaraj Urs's policies had helped backward classes to move up in the state politics. However, the authors come to the conclusion that after 1980 the backward classes have been groping in the dark.

We then move on to Andhra Pradesh. F.D. Vakil surveys the long 35-year period of Congress rule in Andhra Pradesh and makes the point that the gradual decline in the Congress party's "support structure" has resulted in its overthrow. He maintains that all is not yet lost for Congress (I), because it could return to power with an improvement of 6 to 9 per cent in its popular votes. M. Shatrugna analyses the circumstances in which Telugu Desam entered the political scene in Andhra Pradesh and suggests that it is a trend-setter for the political process in our country. He has analysed the caste, educational and age distribution of TDP and Congress (I) candidates. The chapter on the social background of TDP legislators which is a joint effort of three scholars in Hyderabad helps us to understand who got elected. M. Shatrugna and G. Narayana have analysed the caste background, educational qualifications and age of the legislators and have also gone into the details of these aspects, regionwise. G. Srinivas has researched into the 1978 Congress(I) legislators' age, education, occupation, previous political experience, association with co-operative movements, trade unions, cultural organisations and compared these with the similar data regarding the TDP legislators. G. Srinivas's study gives us an insight into the comparative social background of MLAs representing the new party and those MLAs who represented an old party (Congress) in 1978. The authors conclude *inter alia* that a larger number among TDP legislators have higher educational as well as professional qualifications as in medicine, engineering and teaching. This is a notable change from the well-known fact that hitherto lawyers were the largest group of professional in Indian politics.[2] Ratna Naidu researched into an important sociological variable in the elections in Andhra Pradesh, namely, the symbolic imagery used by Telugu Desam. She is of the opinion that although a majority of the voters in the country are not literate, they know their cultural heritage and N.T Rama Rao presented to them the issues in the cultural categories which were meaningful to the people.

The last three chapters analyse the common factors which influenced the elections in both Andhra Pradesh and Karnataka and discuss their implications for the Indian polity as a whole. Amal Ray has linked these elections to "environmental dynamics", namely, changes in spatial levels of political economy, developmental investments, and so on. He sees in the new regional pulls "a highly explosive potential" if they are allowed to "operate in an extremely resource-scarce economy". Bashiruddin Ahmed argues that in both the Andhra Pradesh and Karnataka elections the electorate has put into practice the accountability principle therewith indicating that its support cannot be taken for granted. The new factor emerging from the analysis of the electoral outcome, according to Bashiruddin, was the negation of the elite political culture. This factor has become more powerful than economic or other reasons in influencing electoral behaviour in India. The concluding chapter on primordiality in Indian politics puts forward the case that the flowering of regional culture and aspirations does not necessarily pose a threat to the federal structure at this stage of our social development. It questions the premises of scholars and political activists who maintain that India will disintegrate if people in the different regions assert their identities.

II

A question that may be raised is : How far does money influence a politically conscious electorate? Can financial resources tilt the balance in favour of those who have more?

Money power in elections is an accepted "evil" in a democracy.[3] It has come to a point where we accept the norm that if a party has sufficient resources it can win the election. The premise is that the majority of voters in India are poor and that they seek money or goods in return for their vote for a candidate. Therefore, if a party has enough money, it can buy votes, win the elections and come to power. In other words, what is important in the perception of the voter is not the "performance" of the party in power or the capabilities of opposition parties to perform better than the ruling party. Such a situation makes a mockery of democracy.

On an all-India level the one occasion when the above thesis was proved wrong was the 1977 Lok Sabha elections. Now the 1983 elections at the state levels also has demonstrated that money is not the sole means for winning elections, when other vital issues grip the people's minds. It is common knowledge that Congress(I) which was in power in the two states of Andhra Pradesh and Karnataka had monetary resources at its disposal, while the opposition parties were perhaps not so flush with funds. As *The Week* reported: "The Congress(I) spent an unbelievable minimum of Rs. 10 lakh per assembly segment. Almost Rs. 10 per voter. In certain selected ones—as in Venkatagiri where Janardhan Reddy was contesting—unofficial estimates say that per head expenditure was ten times the average."[4] The Congress(I) contested 515 constituencies (294 in Andhra Pradesh and 221 in Karnataka) and it must have spent a staggering amount of money. The resources of the opposition parties like Janata-Kranti Ranga or TDP were no match to those of Congress(I). Chandrasekhar, the Janata Party President had stated during his *padayatra* that, from the central office of the party, they could not send even Rs. 5000 each to their candidates. Some candidates could not be given any financial support at all.[5] The TDP had said categorically in its election manifesto that "the present trend, where money-power alone wins the elections should go".

In spite of this disparity in financial resources why were people's votes not lured away by the party which spent the maximum amount of money? Does it mean that material incentives cannot any longer play a decisive role in swaying the voters? If this is so, it proves that the electorate is coming of age. The popular saying among the people of Andhra Pradesh was "take money from the hand and run away on bicycle".[6] H.R. Khanna, the former Supreme Court Judge made a perceptive comment on this critical issue:

> One aspect of the Andhra Pradesh and Karnataka elections deserves particular attention. It is said that each candidate belonging to a major political party was paid a substantial sum of money and provided with one or two jeeps for campaigning during the polls. The other candidates do not seem to have enjoyed the benefits conferred by such financial resources. In spite of this disparity, the candidates of the party with ample funds at its disposal fared rather badly. This clearly shows that though money does play an important part in elections, it can be effective only up to a point. If the general trend of public opinion happens to be against a particular party, money cannot tilt the balance in its favour and reverse the prevailing trend.[7]

Money is needed in an election for publicity, travel, meetings, and so on. But in most cases people make the decision for whom to vote according to the issues involved. When the issues at stake in an election are important to the people, they even raise resources locally to support the candidate who, they think, would best represent their cause.

Further systematic research needs to be done on this crucial variable in the electoral behaviour of Indian voters. It is extremely difficult to gather data on the subject, but through "participant observation" in the election campaigns, students of election studies may explore this area which is shrouded in secrecy.

The parties that have come to power respectively in Andhra Pradesh and Karnataka have different political backgrounds. For the second time in Indian politics (the first being M.G. Ramachandran in Tamil Nadu) a cinema star entered politics in Andhra Pradesh and, within a short period of a few months, captured power. Swinging popular feelings is one thing, but governance without previous training or experience as well as without political skill and ideology is quite a different matter. When voted to form governments parties that are not anchored in history and rooted in an ideology will tend to depend on the bureaucracy (including the police) and be surrounded by sycophants. Excessive dependence on the bureaucracy and the police may create a situation where the end result of their actions will be unhelpful to the people in spite of the party leaders' intentions to do good for the people. For instance, in its election manifesto, TDP pledged that "in all circumstances and in all matters it will abide by democratic values and traditions". But within three months of his coming to power the chief minister, N.T. Rama Rao, admitted in an interview that the police might have been violating the citizens' democratic rights. However, he went on to defend the actions of the police saying it was a law and order problem and that it was not in his hands.[8] This raises an important question: What are the political implications of a phenomenon such as the Telugu Desam Movement (TDM) converting itself into a political party within months of its inception and being swept to power? This needs further study on the basis of its origin, political victory and subsequent performance.

Only a party that has an adequate political ideology can bring about structural changes. A semblance of this seems to be taking place in Karnataka. The new government in Karnataka has the backing of a party with a long tradition of political battles; its leaders like Ramakrishna Hegde are experienced politicians. The Karnataka government is avoiding populist measures and facing the hard realities of running a government. No less important are the issues upon which it has focussed its attention, such as centre-state relations, role of the office of governor, attempts to eradicate political corruption, lowering of the voters' age for elections to the local bodies and the setting up of the *Lokayukta* bringing the chief minister also under its purview. The issues have potentials for structural changes and are not merely reformist. In this context, it may be revealing to compare the performance of the state governments of Tamil Nadu and Andhra Pradesh on the one hand and of Karnataka and West Bengal on the other.

One point stressed at the "writers' party" to produce this volume was that the new politics has created a situation where the states may become reference points for the centre in contradistinction to what has been happening so far: that is, till now the centre was the reference point for the states. The appointment of the Sarkaria Commission to review the centre-state relations, the appointment of an expert panel of economists at the centre, the centre's blessings for sharing the waters between Andhra Pradesh and Tamil Nadu through the Telugu-Ganga Project are some instances where the centre recognises the new trends and initiatives in state politics.

But all is not well with the political system. Its pathological nature has come to the surface. This is mainly reflected in the seeming intolerance of the party in power at the centre towards other parties that have come to power in the states. Corrupt and anti-democratic means by which the parties in power try to discredit one another, going to the extent of toppling a party which poses a threat to another are some of the ominous trends. However, there is reason to believe that what is happening today is a churning process in Indian politics and if people retain the ultimate power of being the final judges and assert their will, our polity is poised for a vibrant democratic progress. This is the message of the 1983 elections in Andhra Pradesh and Karnataka.

III

Some major personalities were involved in the shift in Indian politics that is discussed in this book. It is hoped that the profiles of three among them given below will provide the reader with a background, however brief, to what follows:

DEVARAJ URS carved a niche in the hearts of the people of Karnataka with his progressive policies for the uplift of the backward classes. Born in 1915 at Kallahalli (Hunsur Taluk) in Mysore district, he graduated in science from Mysore University. He became an agriculturist. From 1941 till 1948, he was a member of the Mysore Representative Assembly. He participated in the Quit India Movement and in the "Mysore Chalo" struggle for responsible government in 1947. From 1952 until his death on 6 June 1982, he was a member of the State Legislative Assembly and was a minister (1962-67) and chief minister (1972-80). After the Congress party split in 1969 during the historic All-India Congress Committee (AICC) session in Bangalore, Urs was one of the first to support Indira Gandhi. He was appointed convenor of the state ad hoc committee of Congress(R). His support to Indira Gandhi was vindicated when Congress(R) won all the 27 Lok Sabha seats in the state in 1971 and a majority in the State Assembly in 1972. When the Congress party lost power at the centre in 1977, Urs's support helped Indira Gandhi to win a by-election from Chickmagalur Lok Sabha constituency in 1978. Later on, however, he severed his connection with Congress(I) and ranged himself with the opposition, succeeding Swaran Singh as president of the Congress (U). His party lost all but one seat in the 1980 Lok Sabha elections. A few months before his death he founded Kannada-Kranti Ranga, a regional party.

NANDAMURI TARAKA RAMA RAO belongs to the economically and politically powerful Khamma community. Born in 1923 in Nimmakura village in Krishna district, he studied in SRR College, Vijayawada, and graduated from Andhra Christian College, Guntur in 1947. He gave up his post as joint sub-registrar in 1949 and entered the film world. Within a brief period he rose to stardom—his first film being *Mana Desam* (*Our Country*)—and so far he has acted in 292 films. In mythological films he consistently played the roles of avatars. He commanded such great reverence among film-going Telugus that his house in Madras virtually became a pilgrim centre. A strict disciplinarian and teetotaller, he is deeply religious. He is a great fund raiser whenever calamities occur. In 1965 the title of *Nataratna* was conferred on him and in 1968, the prestigious government award, the *Padma Shri.*

While shooting a film in a village near Hyderabad Rama Rao or NTR, as he is affectionately known, was thrown out of a bullock cart and run over. He survived and the accident became a turning point convincing him that his life was spared because he had a mission to fulfil in life. He decided to enter politics after his *Shashtipoorthi* (60th birthday). For 9 months he travelled the length and breadth of Andhra Pradesh in a 1938-model van in which he also slept and which he also used as a platform to address public meetings and street corner gatherings. He launched Telugu Desam on 29 March 1982. The theme of saving the self-respect of Telugus was the party's main plank. For, in the words of NTR: "We have a minister for fish, another for poultry and a third for prawns. We have become a laughing stock in the country. The Congress has 250 members in the house but look at the way they have formed 250 groups, each demanding a post. The people are vexed with this situation. We had lost our self respect and identity and I thought I would go out and tell whoever wanted to listen to me that we are mismanaging this state, that we should behave with dignity so that people in other parts of the country show us the respect due to us". (*The Hindu*, 9 January 1983).

RAMAKRISHNA HEGDE, a lawyer by profession, a writer in Kannada and a lover of agriculture, entered politics at the age of 15 when he interrupted his studies to participate in the 'Quit India' movement and courted arrest twice. His family property was confiscated and seven members of his family, including his mother, were jailed. He was again imprisoned, during the political emergency (1975-77) in Belgaum and Bangalore Central Jails. Born on 29 August 1927 at Siddapur in North Kanara he studied in Kashi Vidyapith and Lucknow University. He was a member of the All-India Congress Committee from 1957 to 1969. After the Congress split he joined Congress(O). Hegde became deputy minister in the Karnataka Government (1957-58) and then cabinet minister in charge of finance, planning, excise, industries, etc. (1962-71). For five years from 1972, he was leader of the opposition in the Karnataka Legislative Council. From the inception of the Janata Party (1977) he was one of its All-India General Secretaries till he became chief minister of Karnataka on 10 January 1983. He resigned from the Rajya Sabha after he was elected with an overwhelming majority to the Assembly on 15 May 1983 from Kanakapura constituency. After his clection victory, Hegde declared that it was the triumph of value-based politics. The statement is significant, for the much-talked about factor about the Janata government in Karnataka was its novel style of functioning in order to introduce "morality" into public life.

Notes and References

1. The first non-Congress ministry in India was formed as early as 1954 by the Praja Socialist Party led by Pattom Thanu Pillai in Travancore-Cochin (Now part of Kerala). After reorganisation of the states (1956), Kerala was again the first state to vote to power a non-Congress government when E.M.S. Namboodiripad became the first Communist chief minister in 1957. After a decade, in 1967, north India (except Rajasthan) followed suit by electing a number of Samyukta Vidhayak Dal (SVD) governments. This was also the time when the Dravida Munnetra Kazhagam (DMK) captured power for the first time in Tamil Nadu. The logical end of it all came in 1977 when the Congress lost power at the centre for a period of some 34 months.
2. "... it would seem that the legal profession has not only maintained but even improved its dominant position in Indian politics and public life over the last three decades in independent India." T.K. Oommen, The legal profession in India: Some sociological perspectives, *Indian Bar Review*, Vol. X, No.1, 1983, p. 5.
3. See for instance the issue of *Seminar* (74) October 1965, on "Money in politics".
4. *The Week*, January 16-22, 1983, p. 6. See also *Sunday*, January 16-22, pp. 23, 33.
5. Chandrasekhar confirmed this in a personal interview. He explained that the total amount he and his colleagues could mobilise at the national level for the entire election was about Rs. 10 lakhs.
6. The Hand was the election symbol of Congress(I) and the Bicycle that of TDP.

7. H.R. Khanna, Funds for the party: Where black is beautiful, *The Statesman*, February 9, 1983.
8. In an interview with a delegation of Andhra Pradesh Civil Liberties Committee (APCLC) and People's Union for Civil Liberties (PUCL), March 19, 1983, Quoted in *NTR's One Year*, APCLC and People's Union for Democratic Rights, January 1984.

2

SOCIAL STRUCTURE AND THE POLITICAL SYSTEM IN KARNATAKA

A Sociological Perspective on the Elections to the Seventh Vidhana Sabha in Karnataka, 1983

K. RAGHAVENDRA RAO

IN EXPLORING tentatively the relationship between the social structure and the political system in Karnataka, as reflected in the results of the recent elections to the seventh Vidhana Sabha in Karnataka in 1983, I shall adopt the following plan. In the first section, I shall make a few general reflections on the political system and the social structure in Karnataka and their relationship. In the second section, I shall go into the possibilities and limitations of understanding this relationship in terms of the recent elections in Karnataka. In the third and final section, I have some "hypotheses"[1] about this relationship to be tested by a more structured and controlled study of the elections in the state.

I

We are attempting a broad picture of the political system in Karnataka, as stipulated in formal documents. A more realistic and functional account will be given in the last section. The formal structure of the political system of

Karnataka derives from the Indian Constitution as amended up to date and the judicial pronouncements at various levels relating to this structure. The first and foremost characteristic of the political system is that it constitutes a systematic part of a larger political system and that its functioning is inter-meshed with this larger political environment. This larger environment sets the limits to the working of the Karnataka political system, and is a source of resources and constraints for that system. One way of defining this situation is that Karnataka is a unit in a larger federal system. However, the nature of this federal environment is problematic, and has led to such ambiguous formulations as "quasi-federation". Another way of putting it is to say that it is a federal system with a pronounced bias towards centralization. Further, it has been maintained that it is either a unitary system in a federal disguise or that it is a federal system with unitary trappings. To add to this ambiguity, perhaps to make this ambiguity more clear, I suggest that our Constitution contains, in fact, two constitutions—one predominantly federal and other predominantly unitary. How exactly the system functions and what are the specific relationships within it, remains an open political question, not a constitutionally petrified issue.

The second basic feature of the Karnataka political system is that it is, in constitutional terms, a parliamentary democracy. From this flow certain consequences. It has an executive that is part of the legislature and is accountable to it and is controlled by it primarily through its control over public finance. The executive is structured as a cabinet or council, based on the principle of collective responsibility but united by the unique position (*primus inter pares*) and leadership of the chief minister. The legislature, bicameral in Karnataka, has a directly elected democratic lower house, the Assembly, which has a constitutional term of five years, and an upper house, the Council, which is indirectly elected, is continuous and not subject to dissolution. While there can be debate about specific rights or privileges, there is no doubt that the lower house is the more decisive house. The upper house is smaller. The lower house is elected by adult franchise through a system of secret ballot. Elections are the heart of the system insofar as it represents the democratic principle of popular sovereignty. This account, however, needs two immediate qualifications. The first is that legislative control of the executive is, in practice, a myth since the executive can manipulate the legislature through the party mechanism, and the opposition finds itself condemned to impotent fury or intemperate and irresponsible criticism.

Though not formally recognised, the political system makes little sense without taking into account the role of the party system. In theory, there is no restriction on parties other than the ruling party, but, in practice, the party system has tended towards what has been termed the one-party dominant system. This means that though all parties have equal chance to capture state power through elections, only one party has managed to do this continuously and consistently. From 1956, when the state came into formal existence as a result of the Parliamentary Act of 1956 which sought to re-organise the Indian states, until the Congress split of 1969, the state has been a clear case of a one-party dominant system. The 1969 split complicated the identity of the Congress party by assigning it to separate parties—Indira Gandhi's Congress(R) and the Congress(O) controlled by a group of old-timers, collectively called the Syndicate. As a result, the control of the state went to the Congress(O). This could be technically construed as a shift from a one-party dominance. In the elections of March 1972, this party was dislodged from power, and the state came to be ruled by the Congress(R). These events indicate certainly a shift from one-party dominance but this was a brief interlude. From 1972 to 1979, it reverted to a one-party-dominant model. For a brief time, the state was ruled by a Congress faction owing loyalty to Devaraj Urs, not Indira Gandhi The total collapse of the Urs Congress in the 1980 elections to the Lok Sabha resulted in the coming to power of the Congress(I) under Gundu Rao. Therefore, it is not quite accurate to say that the 1983 elections brought to an end of Congress rule, for the simple and obvious reason that the pre-split Congress cannot be identified with the different Congress factions. In this sense, the replacement of Congress (I) by the Janata-Ranga or Janata party in 1983 belongs to the post one-party-dominant period inaugurated in 1969.

The political system includes the bureaucracy, which is, in

fact, far more important in the functioning of the system than the members of the bureaucracy or the myths of liberal democracy are prepared to concede. The bureaucracy is the concrete version of the political system with which the people must deal in their day-to-day existence. Moreover, whatever the policy, given the amateur nature of the political leadership in a liberal democracy, it is the bureaucracy which converts policy into any content it may choose. No doubt, the liberal theory demands that the bureaucracy function within a framework of rule of law. But, in practice, the degree to which it may conform to this ideal, depends on the leadership abilities of its political masters and the political consciousness of the ruled.

We have next to nothing by way of source material, on the behaviour of the bureaucracy in Karnataka in the overall context of the political system of the state. We have, no doubt, plenty of impressionistic and untested as well as untestable comment on the corruption and incompetence of the bureaucracy, radiating from the casual and frequent statements and reactions of the ruled.

On the social structure of Karnataka, we have considerable literature in the work of sociologists and anthropologists—M.N. Srinivas on Old Mysore, K. Ishwaran on Bombay-Karnataka, Beals on Hyderabad-Karnataka, M.N. Srinivas on Coorg and Scarlet Epstein on Old Mysore. It is not my purpose here in this limited paper to review this literature. But what is clear, paradoxically, is that the situation itself is far from clear. Three broad patterns emerge. The first is that we have a society in which the caste system is dominant, and within this context one particular dominant caste—Vokkaligas in Old Mysore and Lingayats in Bombay-Karnataka, Hyderabad-Karnataka and Bellary district in Madras-Karnataka. Dominance itself is defined as a composite of different dimensions of dominance—economic, ritual and political. The concept of dominant caste has come in for considerable rough handling by critics, but if employed with caution based on adequate empirical evidence, the concept can be quite helpful. For instance, it does make sense to talk about Lingayat or Vokkaliga dominance in Karnataka at different times, provided we specify this as *political dominance*.

Even then, this sort of formulation raises many problems but it is a good starting point for further analysis. The second pattern is that this is a society in which no single caste can be dominant, and the source of any kind of power will have to be some form of multi-caste alliance. The third pattern is that caste is an insufficient basis for power in this society and other factors such as language, political ideology, personal element and class (whether defined in Weberian or Marxian terms), are also important. For the purpose of this study, I shall assume the following sociological propositions. First, the overall society of Karnataka remains a predominantly caste-dominated system. But this assumption can be misleading unless loaded with a few important riders. One is that we do not find here any *caste system* but merely a plurality of caste groups interacting in the absence of such a system. I have elsewhere characterised this situation as primordial pluralism in contrast to modern pluralism.[2] Further, the social force and relevance of caste is relatively stronger in the rural regions than in the urban centres. But in the urban centres the weakening of caste as a social phenomenon is more than offset by its persistence as a political resource at the service of our liberal democracy. Secondly, it is a social structure characterised by an emerging class system. We have very little material on the class system in Karnataka, and using very general categories one may identify two interlocking systems of class—one in urban Karnataka and another in rural Karnataka. In terms of this rough-and-ready framework, it is possible to talk about an upper class, middle upper class, middle middle class, middle lower class and the poor class. This classification may be cross-fertilised with the more Marxist framework of capitalist class, the middle class (upper, middle and lower) and the working class. In the rural areas, we may speak of a rich peasantry, a middle peasantry, poor peasantry, artisan class, landless labourers and marginal classes such as the lower bureaucratic middle class and the petty money-lending and merchant class. What is most crucial to note in this connection is that the same set of people are involved in both these systems—primordial pluralism and the emerging class system. The third characteristic of this social structure is ethnic/religious pluralism. As against the Hindu majority, there are a number of minorities such as the Muslims. Christians and Jains. But the Jains have become virtually indistinguishable from Hindus. Within each of these groups, there abound further sub-divisions. The fourth characteristic is cultural pluralism. The major element here is, of course, language. Besides the majority Kannada speakers, Karnataka has sizeable numbers of Telugu, Tamil, Marathi and Urdu groups. The Urdu speakers, of course, are identical with Muslims. In short, the social structure is highly diversified, complex and perhaps fragmented. It is, therefore, not surprising that individual behaviour becomes subjected to a bewildering array of identities and loyalties—caste, subcaste, class, subregion, religion, and party.

It is extremely difficult to define what constitutes rational behaviour in such a situation of socio-cultural fragmentation. From the perspective of electoral behaviour, the impact of this social structure occurs as mediated by the party system. Given this social structure, the political parties tend to aggregate as many identities for support as they can. But they may also find it politically advantageous to be selective and concentrate on a few groups, and go all out to capture their electoral support. However, from the perspective of the individual voter, this is a situation that appears to be hopelessly immune to rational decision-making and choice. I hypothesise that a certain irrationality and unpredictability is structurally in-built in this situation. Such rationality as one may salvage arises from the fact that the existence of a multiplicity of groups and factors in the social structure does not preclude the possibility, indeed the probability, of only a small number of these becoming politically and electorally salient in specific constituencies.

Before we launch into the problem of the interaction between the social structure and the electoral process, it is well to bear in mind one or two significant complications in the situations. The first is that the social structure is not a static structure, and it must be seen as moving in a specific direction. I suggest that as Karnataka, in consonance with the rest of the country, becomes increasingly industrialised, urbanised and "modernised", it would be moving in the direction of a predominantly class society and a decreasingly caste society. This would entail that our explanatory strategies must be dynamic, capable of reflecting the dynamics of the social structure under study. While some earlier Marxist explanations tended dogmatically to bypass the *then* still predominant role of primordial social structures like the caste, the more recent non-Marxist explanations have tended to bypass the relevance of class, either because of honest intellectual inertia or a more dishonest ideological motivation masquerading as academic objectivity. In short, for both Marxist and non or anti-Marxist analysts of elections in Karnataka, as in the country as a whole, the problem is to grasp the dynamic, ontologically changing relationship between caste and class. In my view, the increasing thrust must be towards a class-caste framework, in which class may be seen to articulate structurally with caste, the latter becoming increasingly subordinate to the former. In short, caste politics must be increasingly perceived as deflected or distorted or articulated by class politics. The second complicating factor is that we should not regard the impact as a one-way traffic. This means that we should not only concede the impact of social structure on the electoral process, we should also be prepared to concede the reciprocal impact of the electoral process on the social structure. It should be conceded that the very exigencies of the electoral process mobilises individuals and groups in directions away from the existing social structure. The cumulative effect of this process could well be a long-range structural change in society. The classical Marxist model of the socio-economic structure determining ultimately the political superstructure may have to be modified to accommodate some structural manoeuvre on the part of the political superstructure.

II

A problem area in the research in voting behaviour or system behaviour is to interpret this behaviour in terms of the social structure within whose context the electoral process takes place. Given the secret ballot, the theoretical problem of relating votes cast and the social identity of the voters becomes at best a guess in approximation. Nonetheless, this is a worthwhile effort. But what is equally difficult is to establish the sociological causality of voting behaviour. According to one seasoned student of voting behaviour, election results are amenable to only two sorts of interpretations: (1) the establishment of the level of participation in terms of the votes cast, and (2) the number of votes cast for particular parties or candidates, enabling us to establish the distribution of preferences.[3] Since this paper limits itself to available unofficial data only, its findings should be regarded as less rigorous and more commonsensical and experiential in a subjective sense. Yet such findings must be employed to generate heuristic hypothesis or to supplement abstractly objective data with subjective corroborations. It is in this spirit of scientific humility that I propose to plunge into what may appear to be sweepingly imaginative exercises. I shall make the unconfirmed but intuitively reasonable assumption in interpreting the election results, that the social structure of any particular unit may be roughly correlated with the voting pattern in that unit. For instance, if constituency X has community Y as a majority or as the largest single group, and if in that constituency, candidate A wins, it is reasonable to suppose that he could have won only with a significant level of support from community Y. No doubt, this is a simplistic formulation, but I think this is better than pseudo-scientific statistical overskill.

One practical difficulty encountered by anyone trying to relate the social structure of Karnataka to the voting process is the total absence of the relevant census data. The Indian census system does not collect any data about caste groups in general. Only the scheduled caste and scheduled tribe groups are officially enumerated. But there are, however, other sources based on other non-census agencies. For instance, some of the backward classes commissions have estimated their own data on caste demography in the state. Such data, though short of absolute authority, may be accepted for the purpose of broad analysis of the interaction between caste groups and the electoral process.

But before looking at the election data for 1983 in Karnataka, a brief and general historical backdrop is in order. Prior to 1956, when the new state of Mysore, consisting of Kannada-speaking population was formed, we find emerging a clear pattern of political dominance by particular castes in the different subregions of Karnataka. For instance, the Old Mysore area was dominated by the Vokkaligas since they provided the chief ministers and crucial ministerial personnel. After the installation of responsible government in Old Mysore, all the chief ministers until 1956, were Vokkaligas. In Hyderabad-Karnataka, Bombay-Karnataka and a part of Madras-Karnataka (the district of Bellary), the Lingayats were the dominant group in terms of electoral politics. After the creation of the new Mysore state in 1956, the communal balance of political power tilted towards the Lingayats. From 1956 to 1972, the state was ruled by a series of Lingayat chief ministers. But the Vokkaliga and Lingayat dominance should be strictly seen as dominance within a hegemonic alliance of upper caste Brahmins with dominant middle caste groups, supported by the Scheduled Caste groups and Muslim minority under the common umbrella of the Congress party. From this power-holding alliance, the heterogeneous group of intermediate castes, also known as backward classes, were excluded. In Karnataka, under Indira Gandhi's overall strategy, Devaraj Urs pursued a policy of retaining the Scheduled Caste and Muslim components of the old alliance, while jettisoning the upper caste and middle caste groups in the intermediate castes. These were numerically significant, and they were used, to break the political back of the dominant middle castes of Lingayats and Vokkaligas.[4] From 1972 to 1980, it was this alliance that ruled the political roost in Karnataka. However, with Gundu Rao's induction as chief minister with Indira Gandhi's blessings, the earlier alliance suffered some slight crack. Further, some underground tension seems to have arisen between two components of the old alliance—the Scheduled Castes and the backward classes. Thus, the strategy of Indira Gandhi had moved somewhat closer to the older Congress communal coalition that she had opposed in 1972.

In terms of class, we may note (a) an increasing incursion of the rural middle class as against the landlord class into the power structure, (b) a relatively larger presence of rural folk in general, (c) and an increasing incursion of lower middle class into the ruling party's power structure. But this changing pattern of class power was related structurally to the changing pattern of caste alliance dominating state's politics. The two patterns tended to collude into a socio-economic-political power structure.

Assuming that the uppermost caste of Brahmins account for about 4 per cent, Vokkaligas 18 per cent, the Lingayats 20 per cent, the Scheduled Castes and Scheduled Tribes 18 per cent, the Muslims 9 per cent and the intermediate caste groups 31 per cent approximately, one can visualise a wide range of political group alliances forged to secure the majority electoral support. The pre-1972 Congress in Karnataka had worked out one combination, and Urs, under Indira Gandhi's overall command, had worked out another alliance. But till 1983 assembly elections, it was assumed that the primordial groups tended to vote as blocks or, more fashionably, as "vote banks". Any fission within the block or the bank was considered at best marginal. This assumption carried with it further supportive, secondary assumptions. One was that the community constituted a very coherent and integrated unit, with little internal democratization due to the low level of politicization, and therefore, easily amenable to the control of elitist leaders. The second assumption was that caste identity and caste interests were perceived to be blended into a harmonious whole by the community membership. The third assumption was that voting was consciously exercised on the basis of such caste rationality. In short, this theory held that voting was not an act of individual rationality or choice, but of community choice or rationality.

In this conception of the interaction between the social structure and the electoral process, the political party was seen as a mechanism for aggregating block votes available in highly integrated and communalized primordial social entities. What was missing in this model was the assumption that the community leaders and their individual community followers were also bound by an unsophisticated rationality. In this view, the individual may be seen as rational because the communal relationship is given by his life situation. In the absence of a modern cross-cutting social structure, the overwhelming majority of the electorate, located in rural areas and semi-urban small towns saw rationality in clinging to what they found to be the most reliable source of support and security—psychological, socio-cultural, economic and political. The 1983 elections in Karnataka may be arguably and speculatively seen as involving a radical change in this pattern of interaction between the social structure and the electoral process. One could perhaps suggest that this represented a shift from primordial electoral rationality to a more fragmented and "modernized" type of electoral rationality.

III

Before interpreting the sociology of the elections of 1983 in Karnataka, it may be helpful to look at the bare statistics.[5] The total number of voters eligible to participate in the 1983 election to the seventh Karnataka Legislative Assembly was 1,98,36,036 (about 20 million). Of these only 12,919,458 (about 12.9 million) exercised their votes. This works out to 65.131 per cent. The distribution of votes cast and seats won party-wise are summarised in Table 2.1.

The subregional electoral results are presented in Table 2.2. Table 2.1 figures underscore a certain continuity in electoral success pattern, since the Congress(I) has continued to retain its relative superiority in its traditional strongholds of Hyderabad division and Bombay-Karnataka, and its relative weakness in Old Mysore and Coorg-Dakshina Kannada (DK). What should also be noted is that while the Congress(I)'s relative strength in its traditional strongholds has come down slightly, the opposition has registered slight gains in both its traditional strongholds as well as traditionally Congress areas. But when we look at the overall situation in the state as a whole, the Congress(I) continues to be the party with the largest number of votes cast for it. These are pointers against any over-optimistic interpretation of the decline of Congress(I) by supporters of the opposition and objective academic non-partisans.

Even if we exclude methodologically what may be called mediating variables (not the conventional intermediate variables) and assume a simple one-to-one correspondence between votes cast and social composition of the electorate, we need

TABLE 2.1 : **Partywise seats contested, seats won and votes cast in 1983 election in Karnataka**

Sl. No.	Name of party	Contested	Elected	Forfeited deposit	Votes polled	Percentage
1	2	3	4	5	6	7
A.	*National Parties*					
	1. Indian National Congress†	221	82	1	5,221,419	40.42
	2. Indian Congress (Socialist)	19	—	19	17,819	0.14
	3. Janata Party††	194	95	44	4,275,355	33.09
	4. Lok Dal	26	—	26	68,348	0.53
	5. Communist Party of India	7	3	1	161,192	1.25
	6. Communist Party of India (M)	4	3	—	115,320	0.89
	7. Bhartiya Janata Party	110	18	71	1,024,892	7.93
B.	*State Parties*					
	1. Indian Congress (J)*	29	—	29	14,082	0.11
	2. Muslim League	4	—	3	19,327	0.15
	3. All India Anna Dravida Munnetra Kazhagam**	1	1	—	16,234	0.12
C.	*Independents*	750	22	686	1,985,470	15.37
	Total	1,365	224	880	12,919,458	100.00

*State Party in Haryana.

**State Party in Tamil Nadu.

†Includes the seat won by Congress(I) on 27 February, 1983 in Tarikere, earlier countermanded because of the death of the Congress (I) candidate.

††Kannada Kranti Ranga contested under the symbol of Janata Party and after the elections merged with it. However, six Kranti Ranga MLAs under the leadership of Bangarappa kept their separate identity. Janata Party formed government with the support of CPI, CPI(M) and BJP.

Source : Election Commission of India, *Report on the Election to the Office of President of India, 1982 and Legislative Assemblies, Delhi Metropolitan Council, 1982-83*, New Delhi, 1983, p. 78.

TABLE 2.2 : **Sub-regional electoral results (1983) in Karnataka**

(percentage of votes cast in brackets)

Party	Hyderabad division	Bombay-Karnataka	Old Mysore	Coorg-D. Kannada
Congress(I)	22 (44)	26 (43)	29 (38)	5 (44)
Janata and allies	15 (36)	21 (38)	70 (46)	13 (56)
Others	2 (20)	10 (19)	11 (16)	—
Total	39	57	110	18

Note on subregions: Hyderabad division has Gulbarga, Bidar, Raichur and also Bellary districts. Bombay-Karnataka includes districts of Belgaum, Bijapur, Dharwad and North Karnataka. Old Mysore has nine districts: Chitradurga, Tumkur, Kolar, Bangalore, Mandya, Mysore, Hassan, Chikmagalur and Shimoga. Coorg and Dakshina Kannada (DK) subregions are specially contiguous.

Source: Computed from the detailed results of general elections to the Legislative Assemblies 1983 (Provisional) mimeographed, Election Commission of India, New Delhi.

very detailed sociological data for each of the 224 constituencies, and this is not only difficult to get, but, in view of the time and resource shortages, this study has done no such micro-analysis. Therefore, what we are left with is a very broad-based macro picture. Roughly assuming that Hyderabad division and Bombay-Karnataka are Lingayat dominated areas, it appears that the tie-up between the caste and the Congress(I) which had been weakened earlier by Indira Gandhi and Urs, has now been resorted to some extent. At the same time the Janata's marginal increase in support in these areas indicates that some traditional Congress(I) support groups, perhaps the Muslims and Harijans, or even the intermediate caste groups, have found it necessary to switch over their suport to the Janata. Similarly, the opposition success in the other two areas should be taken as overwhelming Lingayat, Vokkaliga, Muslim and Scheduled Caste support for the opposition. In terms of a caste interpretation of electoral politics in the state, this seems to push us towards a paradox. On the one hand, the traditional communal and primordial basis of politics remains substantially intact, but its internal components have been shifting. On the other hand, such shifts do not make any sense exclusively or even predominantly in terms of primordial communal politics. I think future work on electoral process and politics in the state should concentrate on this paradox. This should lead us to such mediating variables as changing relations between caste and class, the changes in each of these variables themselves, the rise of that elusive phenomenon, political consciousness of the electorate, and the increasingly effective mobilizational skill and impact of the parties. These are matters on which, in the absence of hard empirical data, this paper can only indulge in speculations, but these speculations need not be dismissed wholly as idle.

While, as we have already seen, caste remains a significant variable, it is being increasingly weakened because of the needs of the electoral system itself to arrive at multi-caste alliances on the part of the elite strategists and the elite need to reckon with the increasing political awareness of the people, not in sophistication but in quantum. What seems to matter is not that people are becoming more aware of the complex mechanisms of modern democratic politics, but that more people are now conscious of this system in terms of their immediate interests and their simplistic sense of moral values. In this perspective, the political parties have to aggregate not merely primordial caste identities but also immediate interests as well as intangible moral preferences. While all parties may be sharing certain common concerns rooted in the electoral system and its wider political context, they may also have their own ideological positions—left, centre or right—and these may affect the pattern of aggregation, especially with regard to priorities as between primordial identity, immediate material interest and intangible ethical orientation. It may not be unreasonable to suggest that in the electorate's own perceptions, attitudes and motivations, all these three components are enmeshed beyond any analytical recovery. This is to say that we need a composite concept based on the interrelationship between these three components. Perhaps, one needs to fuse perception and motivation, consciousness and action, into a comprehensive explanation of voting behaviour. In such an explanation, the social structure should be assigned a crucial role in terms of whether the electorate accepts its authority uncritically or after critical reflection and conscious choice, or opposes it uncritically or after conscious choice. May be the attempt to get at such apparently invisible variables requires a methodology of micro-intensification and involved attention or participant observation. In short, the present designs in electoral study should be radically re-thought to accommodate categories like consciousness as against attitudes, and action as against voting behaviour as a surface category. Since all this is future agenda, the question remains: what can one say meaningfully on the basis of the existing data? Very little in the sense of rigorously empirical generalizations, but something substantial in terms of imaginative reconstruction. In the concluding summary, I shall do just that—unscientific in the narrow sense but potentially scientific, speculation and reconstruction. based not on the observed, but the unobserved, not on the said but on the silences that haunt our epistemological structures.

Summing up

Given our gaps in knowledge and the complexity of the situation any interpretation of the interaction between the social structure and the electoral process is bound to be both tentative and tortuous. No simple models of voters' rationality or irrationality will do. The question, "Why does the voter vote the way he does?" admits of a variety of responses. But looking from the perspective of the social structure, the question needs re-phrasing as follows: How does the voter's role, position, situation, orientations in regard to this structure, his activities within it and in terms of it determine, if they do, his voting preference? I shall try to answer this question in relation to the overwhelming rural masses first. I think the rural voters are right in assuming that caste identity has a potentially material basis, and hence they tend to vote on caste lines. In other words, they vote a man of their caste, not only because he is of their group, *but also because doing this promotes their material interest*. They may be wrong about assuming this, and, indeed, one way of looking at so-called election surprises or landslides is to interpret them as occasions of this realisation—caste identity and material interest do not *now* hang together. But they do not know how to understand this situation, which they seem to grasp intuitively, subjectively, and existentially. What we have here is not a simple "false consciousness" but a more complex "primitive consciousness". They know something has gone wrong but they are unable to convert this existential perception into an epistemological category. Lacking explanations of a sophisticated, "theoretical" kind, they fall back increasingly on either immediate material interest—local demands for facilities—or they fall back on their simple moral perceptions—this person is good, that person is bad. Of course, one should not minimise the role of active "misinformation" and ignorance. Perhaps one reason why political scientists have not uncovered this pattern is because our instruments of enquiry such as the questionnaires proceed on different assumptions.[6] If we were to re-design them, perhaps something of this pattern of social structure—electoral process interaction might emerge.

A second important conclusion could be that within the existing social structure, the possibilities of their "primitive consciousness" developing into a more objective and genuine consciousness, appear to be limited. So the voter is led to a position of cynicism and indifference based on impotence reinforced by ignorance. They can perceive increasingly the widening gap between electoral promises and governmental performance. In more advanced capitalist systems, the liberal democratic process mutes this impotence and hurriedly papers over this gap by the goodies delivered by the relatively more productive economy. Here the situation is potentially more explosive.

To my mind the overall problem can be formulated in this way. The liberal democratic political system accepts elections *within a given social structure*. The parties and rulers are bound by its rules. There are implicit rules which prevent any policy being pursued that may threaten the foundations of the social structure. In advanced liberal systems, this threat is continually postponed, thanks to the economic benefits. In the absence of co-option by consumerist corruption, in our situation the electorate can only demonstrate a progressive rise in the level of frustration, impotence and anger. What I am really suggesting is that the electoral system and the social structure interact only minimally and superficially, precisely because that is the institutional condition of the electoral process itself. In this perspective, the 1983 elections in Karnataka may be seen as reflecting the social reality, especially the increasing "materialization" of the people's culture and the increasing shift from caste to class via the self, though only to a marginal extent. Elections are not meant to be faithful mirrors of social processes, and their primary function is to gather images in a selective way to uphold and sustain one dominant and selective image of the society. Thank God, the elections occasionally overstep their assigned function in a liberal democracy and respond more actively to the social process. The 1983 elections in Karnataka, and perhaps Andhra, may well be consequences of such overstepping!

Postscript

One comment made on this paper is that I should have also attempted to draw some broad tactical or strategic inferences from my analysis of the situation. Though I then argued that the paper was not originally designed to go into this issue, at least directly, I now feel, on second thought, that a brief note on the issue may be helpful.

The main strategic issue, of course, is not a *politically neutral* issues, since it involves the crucial question: strategy for whom? From whose perspective? For whose benefit? Without going into too much detail, and somewhat oversimplifying the problematic, there can be two broad, and broadly opposed, perspectives, each relating to the interests of two parties. The first is the perspective of the rulers, the ruling class and the ruling elites, who control the political system. Then there can be on the opposite side the rest of the population who constitute the ruled, the managed, the manipulated, the dominated and the exploited—the masses or the "people". The fact that the interests of the two sides are fundamentally and structurally antagonistic, over a long historical range of time, does not rule out temporary and tactical alliances between the groups, and efforts to use the system to promote the *objectives it has been designed not to promote*.

Since I do not propose to be in the first camp, and am committed to the second camp—the camp of the ruled and the overmanaged and the exploited—I do not propose to worry about the problems of the first party, but focus briefly on the plight of the second party. In any case, the first group has enough resources to work out its own historical salvation or, I fondly hope, suicide! As I have presented the situation in the paper, the masses, the bulk of the electorate, have not been able to make any significant use of the system to promote their own interest. I have also suggested that, given the situation of their "primitive consciousness" and the overwhelming resources at the command of the other camp, the political parties representing the interests of the toiling masses, especially the Communist groups, must be resigned, excepting in some areas like West Bengal, Kerala and Tripura, to short-term defeats in the electoral battle. The strategic issue would be: if they cannot conquer political power electorally, then why waste one's limited resources in a futile game in which defeat seems to be guaranteed from the start? To my mind, the revolutionary parties cannot and should not opt out of the game, if for no other reason than that the game affects *physically* large and massive populations. Then the question would be one of priorities and proportions with regard to resources like organization, money, time and morale. There should be an attempt, during the election times, to go all out to deploy *simple human resources*—youth and ordinary men using their bodies and moving into every nook and corner, to educate and mobilise the masses to create "consciousness", convert "primitive consciousness" into a proper consciousness. In short, the strategy should be *to do precisely what the system has been designed to prevent being done.* In other words, their thrust should be to upset the political content of the electoral process as defined in the liberal democratic agenda, by *turning a ritual occasion into a genuine mass activity*. Now, it seems to me that the revolutionary parties and groups indicate that they know that this is what should be done, but their programmes and their praxis, however, do not reflect this strategic consciousness. Of course, one should work to win the elections, but one should continuously attempt to derail the bourgeois electoral train to the advantage of the toiling masses. All this may be commonplace, but a commonplace tends to be *unperceived.* It is necessary to repeat the commonplace, if it is an important commonplace, mechanically, even at the risk of being called stupid.

Some may think that this paper contains "fatalistic" overtones. I think this unease arose out of a confusion between objectivity and fatality. The former is partly fatalistic as historical necessity, but it also contains a component of historical "freedom". The opposite of fatalism is not romantic and adventurist freedom, but it is historically available "freedom" based on a scientific and objective understanding of history. A fatalist is one who cannot perceive the difference between what is historically undeterminable and what is historically yet to be determined. The paper was primarily designed to deal with the historically undeterminable in order to isolate it from the historically "free" space in which subjective options exist.

Notes and References

1. "Hypothesis" is used here in the weak sense, that is, as general observations on the nature of the situation.
2. See my unpublished Ph.D. thesis, "Linguistic Politics and the Congress Party in Mysore, 1947-1956," 1974, University of Toronto.
3. Donald E. Stokes, Voting, in the *International Encyclopaedia of Social Sciences*, Macmillan Company and the Free Press, 1968, Vol. 16, pp. 387-95.
4. This point is further elaborated in Chapter 3 by V.K. Natraj and Lalitha Natraj in discussing Backward Classes, Minorities and the Karnataka elections.
5. *Kannada Prabha*, Bangalore, 23 January 1983.
6. I owe this highly suggestive and promising insight to my good friend, Prof. K.J. Shah, retired Professor of Philosophy, Karnatak University, and currently with Poona University on a special assignment.

SELECT BIBLIOGRAPHY

Berelson, Bernard; Lazarsfeld, Paul F., and MacPhee, William N., *Voting: A Study of Opinion Formation in a Presidential Campaign*, Chicago, University of Chicago Press, 1954.

Butler, David E., and King, Anthony, *The British General Elections*, London, Macmillans, 1965.

Campbell, Angus; Gurin, Gerald, and Warren E. Miller, *The Voter Decides*, Evanston, Row Peterson, 1954.

Ishwaran, K., *Tradition and Economy in Village India*, London, Routledge and Kegan Paul, 1966.

Kothari, Rajni (Ed.), *Caste in Indian Politics*, Bombay, Orient Longmans, 1970.

Lazarsfeld, P.F. and Berelson, Bernard, *The People's Choice*, New York, Columbia University Press, 1966.

Rao, K. Raghavendra, "Linguistic Politics and the Congress Party in Mysore 1947-1956", unpublished Ph.D. thesis, University of Toronto, 1974.

Sills, David L. (Ed.), *International Encyclopaedia of the Social Sciences*, Macmillan Company and the Free Press, 1968, Vol. 16.

Srinivas, M.N., *Caste in Modern India*, Bombay, Asia Publishing House, 1962.

Weiner, Myron; and Kothari, Rajni (Eds.), *Indian Voting Behaviour: Studies of the 1962 General Elections*, Calcutta, Firma Mukhopadhya, 1965.

3

BACKWARD CLASSES, MINORITIES AND THE KARNATAKA ELECTIONS

LALITHA NATRAJ

V.K. NATRAJ

THIS paper attempts an analysis of the 1983 elections to the Karnataka State Assembly from the angle of the backward classes and numerically minor castes and communities. Karnataka elected to power a non-Congress government in 1983, the first ever in the state. This election deserves investigation not for this reason alone although it is significant in itself. It becomes important because in the last decade Karnataka has figured in the limelight as a state which under the stewardship of Devaraj Urs managed to break away from the domination of the two numerically largest caste groups in the state and gave a meaningful place to the minority communities. A discussion of the 1983 election must necessarily be set against the backdrop of the "caste" phenomenon in the state over the last few decades and must also take particular note of the developments during Devaraj Urs's chief ministership. Hence the paper divides itself into five parts. The first part deals with the fight of the non-Brahmin caste groups in princely Mysore. The second part deals with the 1948-1972 phase, the third with Devaraj Urs's policies and the fourth with the 1983 elections. The fifth and concluding part summarises the findings.

I

Karnataka has acquired in the last decade a reputation for being a state that has made distinct strides in mobilising the backward classes and "minority" caste groups to fight the hegemony of economically and numerically dominant castes. This reputation is inextricably linked with the name of the late Devaraj Urs who as chief minister (1972-80) is generally credited with this phenomenon of backward class mobilisation. It is important to remember that caste has played an important role in the state for several decades and studies are not lacking in the field which point to this factor. The erstwhile princely state of Mysore (in popular parlance Old Mysore) consisting of nine districts[1] of the southern part of Karnataka boasts an organised backward class movement from almost the first decade of this century. This movement, influenced by the Justice Party in the Madras presidency was originally anti-Brahmin in orientation and directed essentially at securing more employment for the non-Brahmin castes in service under the state. To begin with, the movement sought to represent the interests of the entire non-Brahmin group (including for a time the Muslims) but inevitably schisms developed and intra-group rivalry began to surface. Inevitably too the beneficiaries of the movement were only a few of the many castes among the non-Brahmins.[2]

The non-Brahmin movement succeeded in having a committee appointed to look into the question of ensuring adequate representation to non-Brahmins in service under the state. This committee of which Sir Leslie Miller was the chairman reported in 1918. The next twenty years saw several debates in the legislative council as also in the press regarding the implementation of the Miller recommendations. Conflicts within the non-Brahmin group also became a little more accentuated although it would not be correct to suggest that open or organised dissention became evident.

The two caste groups which benefited from this movement were the Lingayats and the Vokkaligas. The Lingayats also known as Veerashaivas are a community who follow the teachings of Basava, an eleventh century mystic who although born a Brahmin rebelled against brahmanical orthodoxy and founded a new sect called the Veerashaivas. They are devotees of Siva. Basava's aim was to found a sect which did not recognise any caste barriers. However, the Lingayats contain among themselves at least three major divisions: the Jangamas (priests), Banajigas (merchant class) and *Sadar*, *Nonoba* and Gowda Lingayats (agriculturists). These groups are generally endogamous. In the old Mysore state the Lingayats were the second numerically largest group after the Vokkaligas, but after 1956 when the districts of Belgaum, Dharwar, Bijapur, Raichur, Bidar and Gulbarga joined to form the reorganised state, the Lingayats became the largest group and now account for about 15 per cent of the state's population. They are vegetarians and have a fairly high literacy rate. They were in the forefront of the non-Brahmin movement of the 1920s and 1930s. Different sections among them owe allegiance to different *maths* and intra-caste rivalry is not uncommon.

The Vokkaligas are essentially an agricultural community found in the southern part of Karnataka. They account for about 12 per cent of the state's population. They also took a leading part in the non-Brahmin movement. The Vokkaligas are far less organised in terms of *maths* than the Lingayats nor are there among them so many distinct groups. The main subdivisions are *Gangadikar*, *Marasu* and *Namdhari*. Their literacy level is not as high as that of the Lingayats. Politically they are a powerful lobby.[3]

It is these two communities—the Lingayats and the Vokkaligas—which are generally referred to as the "dominant" or "major" communities in Karnataka. By virtue of this numerical strength plus their considerable economic power they were able to wield a very high degree of influence over the politics of the state in the years immediately following independence. Their leading role in mobilising the non-Brahmins was an advantage, even though the Lingayats and the Vokkaligas did not work together at all times. Ever present was a mutual distrust between them. Both groups established their caste associations in the early part of the century. Of the two, the Lingayats had a head start in terms of establishing educational institutions.

It is necessary to add here that the foregoing should not be taken to imply that these efforts of the Lingayats and the

Vokkaligas helped their communities as a whole. Given the circumstances, it was as inevitable then as it is now that the benefits should have remained by and large confined to a few sections of the two communities but they succeeded in making them politically articulate and influential.

We do not propose to delve further into the history of the backward classes movement for reasons of space. The one other point worth mentioning is that when the non-Brahmin movement was at its height the Scheduled Castes (SCs) (then called Depressed Classes) were hardly in a position to put forward their case and had considerable misgivings about being part of the large amorphous non-Brahmin group. It would be correct to suggest that their interests were in no real sense anyone's concern. All that they got were some token benefits here and there. Incidentally the SCs account for around 11 per cent of the states population.[4] Other caste groups such as the Kuruba, Beda and so on did not make any impression on the state's political arena for a long time. The Kuruba caste has nearly 7.5 per cent of the state's population in its fold. Outside of the Lingayats and Vokkaligas it has probably been the most important group in the non-Brahmin category. Even so it took a long time for the Kurubas to emerge as a real force. However, the Kurubas also had formed their own association at about the same time as the Vokkaligas. Some other numerically minor groups also formed their own associations in the first-two decades of this century but the impact of these groups on the state's politics was not significant.

At this point it is necessary to refer to another dimension of the caste issue in Karnataka. Generally discussion centres on the numerical (and economic) strength of the castes. It would seem to us that a relevant consideration here is the distribution of the various caste groups across the state. For this purpose we present below the spatial distribution of selected caste groups in the nineteen districts of Karnataka. The co-efficient of variation of each of the selected groups is given in Table 3.1.

As will be obvious there is a striking difference between the two major caste groups—the Lingayats and the Vokkaligas. The latter have a high co-efficient of variation (CV) and are

TABLE 3.1 : **Co-efficient of variation of each of the selected groups**

Caste	Total population	% of state population	Co-efficient of variation
1. Agasa (dhobi)	3,55,246	1.18	62.0
2. Darzi	1,11,567	0.37	81.0
3. Devanga (weavers)	2,80,564	0.93	70.41
4. Naviuda	1,91,502	0.64	73.31
5. Beda (Scheduled Tribe)	15,19,620	5.06	99.0
6. Kuruba	20,32,000	6.8	65.45
7. Ganiga	1,56,900	0.52	102.07
8. Brahmin	12,69,450	4.23	72.57
9. Vaisya	1,78,600	0.59	86.40
10. Vodda (declared Scheduled Caste in 10 out of 19 districts)			
S.C.	3,43,775	1.15	82.00
Non-S.C.	1,14,785	0.38	
11. Visvakarma	6,90,690	2.30	42.64
12. Adikamataka (S.C.)	15,74,700	5.37	117.77
13. Adi Dravida (S.C.)	4,64,700	1.59	175.81
14. Idiga	6,75,656	2.25	200.08
15. Lingayat	43,92,700	14.70	87.07
16. Vokkaliga	35,46,170	11.90	124.34

Source : Karnataka Backward Classes Commission (KBCC) Report, 1975, Vol. II.

Note : The KBCC took 1931 as the base year and projected the population of all castes to 1972. The population figures in column 3, therefore, refer to 1972.

concentrated in the districts of Kolar, Bangalore, Mandya, Mysore and Hassan. In the northern parts of the state they are hardly represented. The Lingayats have a commanding majority in the northern districts but have a considerably lower CV than the Vokkaligas. As one would expect, the service castes like the Viswakarma (goldsmith), Agasa (dhobi), Devanga (weaver) and the SCs have a low CV indicating that they are fairly uniformly spread throughout the state. These data are presented with a view to focussing attention on what appears to us a fruitful line of enquiry concerning the role of caste in Karnataka's politics. If we juxtapose the low CV's of the Kurubas and Bedas with their fairly impressive shares in the state's population (nearly 7% and 5.1% respectively) the inference is at least plausible that these represent important emerging forces in the state.

The Scheduled Castes are just over 13 per cent of the population and their distribution is quite uniform. However, there are some important caveats to be entered here so as to see the SCs in the correct perspective.

In the first place, contrary to lay conception, the SCs are not one monolithic block. Primarily there are two divisions among them—the "right hand" and "left hand" SCs. The former engage mainly in agricultural labour (the landless variety) while among the "left hand" we find those who work as cobblers and in similar professions. Many right hand groups such as Holayas have done considerably better for themselves as compared with the left hand groups like the Madigas. The right and left hand groups are endogamous and quite often they do not even interdine. The problem is further complicated by the fact that there are some SC groups like the Lamanis which are touchable Non-Scheduled Castes. In terms of ministerial office and also number of legislators the right hand groups have tended to dominate the scene. While other caste groups perceive the SCs as a monolithic group, perceptive SCs are only too well aware of the division among themselves.

The Dalit Sangarsha Samiti (DSS) is a radical Dalit organisation which is making a determined effort to unify the divisions among the SCs and also bring within its fold the other economically downtrodden groups. The DSS is also acutely aware of the dangers of these divisions among the SCs. Some Harijan leaders are also attempting to put pressure on the state government to delete the touchable SCs from the list. While this effort has not borne fruit so far, it is indicative of the problem. For several obvious reasons the DSS is not able to attract a large following. It is committed to the benefits of reservation being given only to first generation claimants. It is openly critical of Harijan MLAs and MPs who have alienated themselves from the community. This strategy of trying to represent not merely the SCs but also other economically poorer sections does not appeal to all SCs.

It has not been possible to calculate the CV for the different groups in the SC category. However as a whole the SC group is well distributed throughout the state.

Among other groups the Kurubas have not only a sizeable number but are very well distributed. Table 3.1 shows their low CV. So are the Bedas a tribe now scheduled. They are around 5.1 per cent of the state's population and have quite a low CV. The Brahmins, about 4.25 per cent of the state's population, have a good distribution too.

II

Against the backdrop described in the sections above we now turn to the two phases in Karnataka politics that are of direct relevance to this paper. The first phase is from 1948 to 1972 and the second from 1972 to 1980. The first phase may be described as the Lingayat-Vokkaliga hegemony when these two dominant castes called the tune in the state politics. During this period the state had seven chief ministers—three Vokkaligas (K.C. Reddy, K. Hanumanthiah and Kadidal Manjappa) and four Lingayats (S.N. Nijalingappa, S.R. Kanthi, B.D. Jatti, and Veerendra Patil). The Vokkaligas were in overall control between 1948 and 1956. After the enlarged state came into being in 1956 the Lingayats dominated the scene. The threat of Lingayat domination was foreseen by quite a few political leaders and some, for this very reason were opposed to the idea of the enlarged state. Devaraj Urs, in those days only an MLA, was one of those who felt the Old Mysore state was compact and viable. It is more than likely that Urs foresaw what would happen and this was at least part of the reason for his lukewarm attitude to the enlarged state. K. Hanumanthiah on the other hand, welcomed the enlarged state although he should have known that this would mean the end of his chief ministership and would push his community (Vokkaliga) to a secondary position.

In spite of the rivalry between the Lingayats and Vokkaligas, the two maintained an uneasy alliance in so far as shutting out others from the centre of power was concerned.

Actually between 1948 and 1956 and between 1956 and 1972 any threat to incumbent chief ministers emanated mainly from their own caste, the Vokkaligas in the former case and the Lingayats in the latter. For example, Hanumanthiah was manoeuvred out of office just prior to the state's reorganisation in 1956 and his place taken by another Vokkaliga, Kadidal Manjappa. Similarly Nijalingappa the first chief minister of the new state, faced problems mainly from his own Lingayat community.

Two instances of interest could be cited in this context. In 1956, Kadidal Manjappa had succeeded Hanumanthiah as chief minister. The general elections were due in February 1957. But with the reorganised state being created on 1 November 1956 the Lingayats were anxious that Nijalingappa should become chief minister. Some others, Devaraj Urs among them felt that for the remaining few months Kadidal Manjappa could continue. But the Lingayat lobby had its way and Nijalingappa became chief minister on 1 November 1956. Almost immediately Nijalingappa faced problems when some sections of the Lingayat wanted him replaced by Jatti.

The second instance relates to the 1962 general elections. Nijalingappa lost in the elections and therefore S.R. Kanthi another Lingayat was elected leader, but it was clearly understood that as soon as Nijalingappa got into the assembly through a by-election Kanthi would step down and make way for S. Nijalingappa. However, when Nijalingappa got into the legislature Kanthi showed an extreme reluctance to vacate office. It is said that Nijalingappa was so depressed by the turn of events that he was on the point of quitting the ring and stayed on only because of the persuasion of men like Devaraj Urs.[5]

What this illustrates is that during the period of Lingayat-Vokkaliga domination, there was more than a little internecine fighting in the two groups. There was obviously a cordial mistrust of each dominant group by the other. But the common ground between them appears to have been the need to prevent any other caste or community in the state from gaining access to power. Almost right through this period the cabinet contained some SCs and very few from the numerically smaller castes and communities.

One important development that deserves mention is the appointment of the Mysore Backward Classes Committee under the chairmanship of Dr. R. Nagan Gowda in 1960. The reason for appointing this committee was that several government orders issued between 1956 and 1959 in respect of reservation under Arts 15(4) and 16(4) of the constitution were declared void by the courts. The Nagan Gowda Committee quickly produced an interim report based on which came a government order which reserved 22 per cent of the posts for Other Backward Communities (OBCs) and 18 per cent for the SCs and STs. The final report of the committee divided the OBCs into two categories—backward and more backward. The former would enjoy 21 per cent reservation in employment and the latter 24 per cent. In education the percentage of reservation was to be 28 and 22 respectively, (all exclusive of SCs and STs). Caste was the determining factor. To this was added the average enrolment of each community in the last three years of the high school classes and this was compared to the state average. The state average was worked out at 6.9 per 1000.

Nagan Gowda Committee's final report opened a hornets' nest. Based on this a government order was issued in July 1961. While the committee had treated both the Lingayats and the Bunts (the latter are concentrated in South Kanara) as forward, the government order treated them as backward. The logic behind this apparently, was that the committee was not unanimous in regard to these two groups. In actual fact, there was a note of dissent only with regard to the Lingayats by one member, M.S. Patil, himself a Lingayat. The government order stated that the Lingayats were largely rural, engaged mainly in agriculture and manual labour and that they suffered from poverty and illiteracy. It also stated that the Bunts were largely indistinguishable from the Vokkaligas. But after adding these two to the backward list the government order reduced the total extent of reservation to 30 per cent, since 50 per cent as recommended by the Committee was not in the larger interest of the state.

By far the most interesting part of the government order was in relation to the educational level of different castes. The committee had estimated the Lingayat level at 7.1 per 1000 and the state average at 6.9 per 1000. The government order raised the state average to the nearest integer namely 7 per 1000, and decreased the Lingayat average by 0.1 per cent thus leading to the inference that the Lingayats were below the state average.

In 1962 there came another government order which superseded all previous orders. Here the Nagan Gowda Committee's recommendation of 50 per cent reservation for all OBCs was followed. In other words between July 1961 and July 1962 the government quite comfortably resiled from its earlier lofty stand that a reservation of 50 per cent for the OBCs was not in the larger interest of the state. Also while the Lingayats were manoeuvred into the backward category (as described above) some other groups—the Satanis and Nayars for instance whose educational average was just 7 per 1000 were shown no such favour.

The reason for all this is not far to seek. After 1956 political power had effectively passed into the hands of the Lingayats and it would have been a very bold step if the Lingayat demand for the privilege of being declared backward were ignored. The inclusion of the Bunts was patently a step to woo South Kanara. At that time this area had not thrown up leaders of any consequence from other communities like the Billavas which today are quite vocal.

The July 1962 government order was challenged in the Supreme Court in *Balaji versus State of Mysore.*[6] The petition was allowed and Justice Gajendragadkar speaking for the court said that while caste was a relevant factor in determining backwardness it could not be the sole criterion. The whole procedure for making possible the inclusion of Lingayats among the backward classes was 'manifestly erroneous'. The court also observed that 68 per cent reservation was excessive (18 for SCs and STs and 50 per cent for OBCs). An interesting observation made by the court was that caste as a criterion was not applicable to the Lingayats since they contended that they did not follow the Hindu four-fold *varna* classification.

The Supreme Court's judgment in the Balaji case put the state government in a quandary. In order to get over this there came yet another government order which sought to use occupation and income as the criteria for determining backwardness. One other point which needs to be mentioned is this. It is said that in the Balaji case the Supreme Court was prepared to allow the state government's list of OBCs to stand provided the Lingayats were deleted from the list (by applying the doctrine of severability) but that the state government was not ready to accept this. There may be a grain of truth in this but the judgment contains no reference to it.

Any survey of the developments of the 1960s must necessarily lead to the conclusion that the entire debate centred almost exclusively on the position of the upper crust of the OBCs. In the main it concentrated on the Lingayat-Vokkaliga combination. The SCs and STs, got their 18 per cent and thereafter no one appeared to give them a second look. The intermediate groups, the numerically small groups, figured nowhere at all.

The Lingayat-Vokkaliga hold appeared so strong that few, if any foresaw any possibility of a change in this pattern of dominance. But a change did occur and owed itself, literally to a constellation of factors.

At the macro-level there was the split in the Congress in 1969 after which the party in Mysore (as it then was) remained with Nijalingappa and became the Congress(O). The then Congress(R) initially had little support in the legislature which is why Veerendra Patil's Congress(O) ministry could continue in office till 1971 when President's rule was imposed on the state.

These were the years of the Indira wave. Her slogan of *garibi hatao* (end poverty) and her championing of the cause of the weaker sections made a strong impact in the state. It should be remembered too that by this time the Scheduled Castes were beginning to get more vocal partly due to Indira Gandhi's populist and vociferous advocacy of their interests and partly because to some extent at least the protective discrimination practised for more than a decade and a half had achieved some results. With the split in the Congress leading to a large number of the dominant castes remaining with Congress (O), the pitch was ready for the entrance of the minority groups.

III

It is here that Devaraj Urs stepped in to play an important role. It is necessary to furnish a brief background to the career of the man who played a significant role in altering the face of the state's political situation. Devaraj Urs hailed from the Arasu community which accounts for about 0.07 per cent of the state's population and is almost exclusively concentrated in the district of Mysore. The royal family of Mysore belongs to this community. In pre-independence times the community enjoyed palace patronage to the hilt and later, when deprived of this protective umbrella, fell on not very good times. It has produced very few politicians of any repute or importance. Its connections with the royal family were not a great help to men like Devaraj Urs.

Devaraj Urs was in politics right from his student days. From 1942 up to his death in 1982 he represented his constituency (Hunsur in Mysore district) first in the representative assembly and always with an impressive margin. His assembly constituency was altered several times but Urs claimed that this only served to get him better acquainted with roughly half the district of Mysore. Up to 1978 he was the only legislator from his community. His uninterrupted electoral successes obviously gave him enormous self-confidence and in any case he had little else to fall back upon such as the support of an important caste group for example.[7]

Coming from the upper strata in caste as well as class terms [although the Arasus are officially included under the OBCs for purposes of reservation under Art. 15(4)], Urs did not suffer from a feeling of alienation but he was for a long time bypassed for office. His claim was that "by temperament" he was indifferent to caste. While this was true in the sense that in his personal life he was not obsessed by it, in politics he was always a keen student of caste. Nor was he unwilling to use it as a weapon in furtherance of his general interests.

In his early days as an MLA Urs enjoyed a certain luxury in being aloof since he belonged to neither dominant caste. From his own statements made in personal interviews with the authors he said that practically everyone felt free to share confidences with him. Of course a small group set out to keep him at bay possibly because they saw in this quiet man a dangerous adversary. This may be why he was denied office until 1962 when he became minister for transport. After the 1967 general elections also he was in the ministry but he resigned apparently over the allocation of portfolios. According to Urs this also helped him because he toured the state extensively and built up in his own quiet way a following for himself.

After the Congress split in 1969 he joined the Congress(R) which then had few top names in the state. Taking the cue from the prevailing atmosphere and drawing lessons from his own perceptive analysis of the politics of the state and in particular the influence of caste, Urs slowly built up the party. He was, of course, greatly helped by the Indira wave. The party won a resounding victory in the 1971 parliamentary elections. Some associates of Urs who later parted company with him argue that this victory was hardly to be attributed to Urs and should properly be ascribed to Indira Gandhi's charisma. Some even suggest that the Congress(R) victory in the 1972 assembly elections was also largely due to the Indira wave and that Urs could not claim much credit for it as he was unable to do much after he broke away from Indira Gandhi.

Granting that both these propositions are correct there is no gainsaying the fact that Urs showed remarkable political acumen during the 1972 elections. He did not contest then but chose to remain president of the party thus retaining tight control over the selection of candidates. He managed to select candidates from castes and communities which hitherto had remained virtually unrepresented in the legislature. The number of candidates from what are popularly known as the "minorities" increased appreciably. As stated above Indira Gandhi's political posture of the time helped create an environment which was ready to receive the prescription of Urs. The minority groups in the state which had for long sullenly and silently resented the Lingayat-Vokkaliga hegemony found their spokesman in Urs. In espousing the cause of the minority groups Urs was careful not to antagonise the major communities completely. He was too astute a politician to do so. He did two things of interest in this context. He underplayed the importance of the Mandya district, the traditional stronghold of the Vokkaligas. It is said that the party was not anxious to have too many MLAs from this district. Among the Lingayats Urs distributed his largesse rather more generously to the Sadar Lingayats who, again quietly had chafed under the domination of the Jangamas and Banajigas (a description of the caste/class system among the Lingayats is given above).

It is during this period that several minority group leaders gained their entry into the vortex of state politics. A few months after assuming office as chief minister, Devaraj Urs appointed the Karnataka Backward Classes Commission (KBCC) in December 1972. This was no accident. It has already been mentioned that a constellation of circumstances helped bring the issue of the backward classes to the fore in the early seventies. Some leaders of the backward classes (representing mainly the non-Vokkaliga group) seized on the opportunity of a "minority" leader like Urs being the chief minister to press their claims for access to political power. The KBCC was a much bigger affair than any previous commission of a similar kind. Its most important feature was that it had as chairman a very articulate and keenly perceptive student of the backward classes phenomenon in L.G. Havanur. Havanur shared with Urs deep misgivings about the role of the dominant castes and had organised conferences of the backward classes even before Urs came to power. He was, as he is now, a lawyer by profession and had sought the permission of the Supreme Court to intervene in the Chitralekha case[8] but the court did not permit him to do so. Havanur had organised several conferences on the question of backward classes and protective discrimination.

The KBCC had seven members, all of them from numerically small castes. The composition was as follows:

L.G. Havanur—Chairman	—Bedia
Y. Ramachandra	—Kuruba
K.M. Naganna	—Devanga
K.R.S. Naidu	—Balija
Masaner Setty	—Uppara
P.T. Habib	—Darji
Dharam Singh	—Rajput

The commission undertook a comprehensive survey and projected with the 1931 census as the base, the 1972 population of almost all castes in the state. It invited caste associations and groups and individuals to tender evidence and submit memoranda. From its inception the KBCC made an impact on the public mind not the least because its chairman was at all times vocal in expressing unambiguously his view of the backward class problem. The commission submitted its report in November 1975. It listed 15 backward communities, 128 backward castes and 62 backward tribes. In addition, it mentioned 396 castes, communities and tribes whose population could not be ascertained. The criteria for determining backwardness were income, education, occupation, caste and ritual status. It suggested the following percentage of reservation.

Backward communities	16%
Backward castes	10%
Backward tribes	6%
Total	32%

This plus 18 per cent reservation for SCs and STs would keep the total quantum of reservation at 50 per cent thereby following the Supreme Court's view in the Balaji case that reservation above this would be excessive.

One of the most significant points was that the Lingayats and Bunts were both declared forward groups. This deprived the Lingayats for the first time since the beginning of reservation of the privilege of backwardness. As we shall see below, this created a furore which continues even to this day.

The Havanur Report (as it is popularly referred to and often unpopularly) included the Vokkaligas among the backward communities. It is difficult not to heed the criticism that the commission made a political rather than a well reasoned recommendation in this respect. In other words the commission dared not exclude both the dominant communities at the same time from the OBC list. Also it served to create a division between the two which of course was always smouldering under the surface. It is also interesting to observe that the

Havanur report recommended 16 per cent reservation for the backward community group consisting of just 15 communities among which the Vokkaligas easily account for more than 50 per cent of the population in that group.

The most important contribution of the Havanur Report is the consciousness it created among the OBCs. While this was obviously not the doing of his report alone, it played a crucial role at the appropriate time in making the OBCs specially the non-Vokkaligas, conscious and in mobilising them, to press their claims for a greater voice in the state's politics.

Devaraj Urs made some changes while implementing the Havanur report. First, the government included the Muslims among the backward communities. This in spite of an express statement in the Havanur report that Muslims should be treated as a religious minority and not be given the benefit of reservation under Arts. 15(4) and 16(4). But Muslims are about 11-12 per cent of Karnataka's population and the government order on the Havanur Report was issued in March 1977 just prior to the parliamentary elections.

Secondly, the government order brought in a new category called the backward special group. Entry into this group is determined on the basis of occupation and income without reference to caste. Fifteen per cent of the jobs and places in educational institutions are reserved for this group. This was an astute move since it mollified to a certain extent the degree of reservation recommended by the Havanur report. Also it reflected in some way Urs's own philosophy, in his own words "in future we should cut across caste".[9] With this move Urs could claim that his government had given due importance to the economic factor in determining backwardness.

Thirdly, the government order imposed an income limit on those seeking reservation under the backward community and backward caste categories. While a great deal of falsification takes place in income certificates, on the face of it the Urs government could cite this as yet another example of combining caste and economic status to determine backwardness.

The KBCC's work and the report produced several consequences of interest. There was a dramatic proliferation of caste associations and revival of those dormant or moribund, rallies and conferences of backward classes etc. As a result

one could see from 1972 onwards the emergence of political leaders from groups such as the Billavas of South Kanara, the Idigas, the Kurubas and so on. It is during this phase that names which are well known today made their first impact. Gundu Rao, Veerappa Moily, Kagodu Thimmappa, L.G. Havanur himself even Bangarappa to some extent—all these owe their entry into political life on a meaningful scale to the policies of the Urs government.

In political terms the striking effect was that the Lingayat-Vokkaliga hegemony was disturbed. The OBCs could no longer be ignored. They became full participants. It would be incorrect to exaggerate this and suggest that Urs was able to break the Lingayat-Vokkaliga hold on the state once and for all. He managed to break the myth that the major caste domination would continue for all time and helped create an ethos in which other castes felt relatively confident. But he was too intelligent a politician to alienate the Lingayats and Vokkaligas completely. The latter continued to enjoy the status of a backward class but Urs cleverly underplayed the importance of their traditional centre—the prosperous irrigated district of Mandya and sought Vokkaliga support from areas where they did not enjoy such numerical preponderance. It is even suggested that Urs was not too keen on his party winning a large number of seats from Mandya district. As for the Lingayats Urs, wooed the Sadar Lingayats who had always felt somewhat neglected in the early days. James Manor[10] suggests that the Land Reforms Act of 1973 which abolished tenancy and conferred ownership rights on actual cultivators benefited to the Sadar Lingayats. In the absence of reliable data it is difficult to accept this interpretation wholesale and there are others who contest it altogether. But there is considerable truth in the argument that Urs showed the Sadars some preference.

On the whole Devaraj Urs quite successfully projected the image of a leader of all these castes and communities which in the years before his rise to power were relegated to a position of oblivion. However, it is necessary, indeed imperative to subject, the new configuration created by Urs's government to closer scrutiny to test its real strength.

The first point which needs to be made is that Urs suffered

from somewhat hazy notions regarding the caste-class nexus. He elevated the caste battle to the loftier heights of a class war. He would quote Namboodiripad (EMS) statement made in a speech in Bangalore that caste and class do coincide at certain points. Of course the rest of EMS' analysis of class was generally left carefully untouched. In a meeting in 1980 soon after he resigned as chief minister Urs said that one of the basic differences between him and Mrs. Gandhi centred on the question of class. Despite all his perception he was not able to see clearly the importance of the economic base in socialism in contra-distinction to its counterpart in capitalism.

Secondly, even during his stewardship the new alliance he had built up showed signs of fragility. One instance illustrates this quite vividly. In 1973, B. Basavalingappa, a Harijan minister, made a speech in which he criticised Kannada literature. He described it mainly as "cattle fodder" (*Bhoosa* in Kanada). Basavalingappa was often in trouble for his intemperate statements regarding the exploitation of Harijans. He was largely responsible for ending the horrible practice of carrying night soil on the head. But his *bhoosa* speech invited trouble in avalanche proportions. Almost everyone was up in arms against him. Particularly aggressive was the opposition of the Vokkaligas. This could be explained in terms of the cultural proximity between the two and also of the land relation existing specially in southern Karnataka where Vokkaligas are land owners and Harijans mainly agricultural labourers. When the agitation reached quite serious proportions Urs, coolly removed Basavalingappa from the cabinet. While any chief minister might have done the same it shows that the Urs formula appeared stronger than it actually was. Of course at a later stage Urs took Basavalingappa back into the cabinet.

There are those who question whether Urs succeeded at all in achieving an alliance between the Dalits and the OBCs. Their argument is that had this been the case the Dalit movement would not have been born during this phase. It would not be correct to suggest that Urs's policies by themselves produced the Dalit movement. For this would imply that his policies had an anti-Dalit slant. What appears to us is that Urs's policies did little to alter the basic equation in land

relations. The land reforms Act which he brought in, progressive though it was did not touch the landless agricultural labourers. By implication it did not touch the Harijans. Also his policies, coming at the time they did, raised the consciousness of the SCs and STs and other previously neglected groups. This awakening should largely be regarded as having inspired the Dalit movement. The Basavalingappa episode acted as a major catalyst.

Another episode, less known, is how Devaraj Urs was not prepared to appoint Havanur to the chairmanship of a public undertaking since Urs felt Havanur would not be acceptable as he was critical of Brahmins in his report.

One further point in this connection is that some of the first people to desert Devaraj Urs after his break with Indira Gandhi were men from the non-dominant groups—Gundu Rao, Moily, Bangarappa, Kagodu Thimmappa.

Yet when all is said and done, it has to be accepted that Urs did succeed in creating a new awareness. His contribution should be measured in terms of the fact that today everyone swears by the Urs formula and that the OBCs can no longer be taken for granted. We have been at pains to point to the fragility of some of Urs's policies in this direction only to avoid suggesting, as is often misleadingly done, that Urs changed the entire structure of politics in Karnataka and that too irrevocably.

IV

After the resignation of Devaraj Urs some subtle, hardly perceptible, yet important, changes began to take place. An alliance of an ephemeral kind began to emerge among the forward groups—Brahmin, Bunt and Lingayat. Some joint conferences were also held. The Lingayats went further and spoke warmly of the Gundu Rao government. At the same time they began making serious efforts to have the Havanur Report's recommendations altered. Even in the pre-Gundu Rao days Lingayats had argued that their population was grossly underestimated by the Havanur Commission and that they should have been included among the OBCs. This demand of theirs gained momentum after Gundu Rao's government came

to power. The Lingayats also organised a campaign to have all Lingayats register themselves in the 1981 census as Lingayat or Veerashaiva and not Hindu. Their claim was that they were not Hindus but constituted a separate religion by themselves. Although the Gundu Rao government contained quite a few OBC leaders from minority castes the impression that was created was that this government was inclined to be a little more sympathetic to the major communities. In fact one of the first intra-party fights related to the dispute between Gundu Rao and Bangarappa. To checkmate the latter, Rao inducted into the cabinet Kagodu Thimmappa who like Bangarappa comes from the Deevaru community in Malnad (toddy tappers traditionally). Ultimately Bangarappa resigned from the ministry. Later when Devaraj Urs founded his new party, the Kranti Ranga, he joined it and now leads it.

The Janata party in Karnataka was generally identified with the major communities. To the public it seemed to stand somewhat in contrast to the position of Devaraj Urs. But once Urs broke from Indira Gandhi in 1979 the Janata attitude towards him began to change. After he resigned from office there were even rumours that his (then) party, Congress(U) might merge with the Janata. Devaraj Urs himself appeared reluctant to take any decision and most of his supporters drifted back into the Congress(I) fold. A few months before his death he founded the Kranti Ranga. When the elections to the assembly were announced late in 1982 neither the Congress(I) nor the Janata seemed fully prepared for them. Quite a number of parleys were held by the Janata and Kranti Ranga leaders to forge a unified opposition to the Congress(I). It was at this time that everyone began speaking in terms of the Devaraj Urs formula. Actually even a few months prior to the announcement of the elections opposition leaders were busy eulogising the late Devaraj Urs. It looked as if the Janata party had realised the urgency of attracting the backward classes minority vote.

After the election calendar was announced the usual frenetic scramble for tickets began. Whereas Devaraj Urs when he led the Congress was particularly careful in choosing candidates and in giving due representation to the OBCs and the minorities such a careful exercise did not seem to have been

made by Gundu Rao and company. Urs always knew that his continuance in office largely depended on how much support he could muster from these groups without totally alienating the dominant communities. Gundu Rao and his associates apparently did not realise this. Nor did they appreciate the high degree to which their traditional support was eroded. The other important factor is that no party had a leader with the acumen and appeal of Devaraj Urs. As the campaign got underway the Congress(I) found it hard to present itself as the champion of the backward classes. The Janata Ranga combination appeared to play this role with a little more comfort. As stated earlier some Congress leaders openly declared after the elections—L.G. Havanur for instance—that the Congress(I) paid a heavy price for departing from the Devaraj Urs formula of fielding a large number of candidates from the minority castes and communities.

It is interesting that out of the 81 seats won by the Congress(I) the Lingayats and Vokkaligas accounted for 46. The OBCs minus the Vokkaligas accounted for just 23. Out of the 95 Janata-Kranti Ranga seats the Lingayats won 32 and the Vokkaligas 23.

Further, taking the 35 reserved constituencies the Janata won in 18. The Congress(I) lost 13—12 to the Janata and 1 to an Independent. Several prominent Harijans became casualties. C.M. Armugam in K.G.F., ex-Congress minister Renuka Rajendran in Chikkaballapur, P. Venkataramana Social Welfare minister in T. Narasipur in Mysore district, B. Basavalingappa in Bangalore district—these are prominent. In the first-three cases the Dalit Sangarsh Samiti contributed to the Congress defeats in no small measure.

In the previous assembly, there were over half a dozen Muslims. In the 1983 elections only two were elected, one each from the Congress(I) and Janata.

One obvious inference is that the electorate has been quite choosy and merciless in rejecting those whose record as a legislator was poor.

As far as the backward class-minority vote is concerned there does not appear to be any particular geographical pattern. Table 3.2 presents the districtwise performance of the Congress and Janata in the 1978 and 1983 elections.

TABLE 3.2 : **The districtwise performance of the Congress and Janata in 1978 and 1983 elections**

	Congress (I)		Janata	
	1978	1983	1978	1983
Bangalore	9	3	16	23
Kolar	12	5	0	2
Mysore	11	5	4	8
Bellary	9	5	0	4
Kodagu	3	2	0	1
Shimoga	9	1	1	6
Mandya	1	4	8	4
Chitradurga	9	4	1	6
Chikamagalur	5	1	1	4
Hassan	5	3	3	5
Tumkur	11	2	2	6
Raichur	11	8	0	1
Gulbarga	8	5	3	6
Bijapur	7	9	7	3
Bidar	4	4	1	1
South Kanara	11	3	3	3
North Kanara	4	2	2	3
Dharwar	12	7	5	6
Belgaum	10	8	2	5

It will be seen that in the old Mysore area the Congress(I) performed miserably. Mysore, Hassan, Shimoga, Chikamagalur, Tumkur proved disastrous for the Congress(I). In Dharwar and Mandya Congress (I) and Janata did equally well. Bellary showed a marginal preference for the Congress(I) and Chitradurga likewise for Janata. The Congress(I) performed better than the Janata in Bidar, Raichur, Belgaum, Bijapur and Kolar. Bangalore went overwhelmingly to Janata. South Kanara went the BJP way giving it 8 out of 15 seats, Congress(I) and Janata got 3 each. Looking at the distribution of selected castes in these districts it is difficult to discern any pattern.

Some guesses, however may be hazarded with the all important qualification that they are subject to being sustained by micro-level data. Even in districts where the Congress(I) has done better than the Janata, namely Bidar, Raichur, Belgaum, Bijapur and Kolar, its performance in 1983 compares unfavourably with its performance in 1978. Only in Bijapur has it improved on its 1978 performance winning 9 seats in 1983 as against 7 in 1978. It is interesting that in Bidar, Bijapur, Belgaum and Raichur the Lingayat population is quite high. The percentage figures are respectively 14.6, 29.2, 23.1 and 16.0. But Kolar does not fit into this pattern since the Lingayat population is less than 2 per cent of the total. In Dharwar also the Congress (I) fared better than the Janata marginally (7 against 6) but compared to 1978 there is a steep fall (from 12 to 7 seats) and in Dharwar the Lingayats are about 31 per cent of the district population. In Shimoga Lingayats are about 21 per cent of the district population and here Congress(I) won only one seat (as against 9 in 1978). In contrast to this Congress(I) won only 1 seat in Mandya in 1978 and 4 in 1983. In this district there is a heavy concentration of Vokkaligas who form around 52 per cent of the population. Also in Chikamagalur and Chitradurga where the Lingayats are in a strong position (nearly 19 and 22 per cent of the district population respectively) Congress(I) has not done all that well.

On the whole the one factor that seems to stand out is the shift of the SC vote from the Congress to Janata. As far as the non-Vokkaliga OBCs are concerned they appear to have shown a marginal preference for Janata. It can certainly be said that both the SCs and the OBCs have overcome whatever mistrust they may have had of the Janata. To this extent the Janata invoking the name of Devaraj Urs has paid handsomely. With a little exaggeration we might say that the spirit of Devaraj Urs has quite considerably influenced this election.

Post-election developments have shown the basic weakness of the backward classes and minorities, namely, their relative lack of self-confidence and their inability to stick together. In the leadership struggle which started after the elections Bangarappa seemed intractable. However, his version is that he was cheated out of the chief ministership even though he had contributed significantly to the victory of the Janata-

Ranga and the Janata national leaders had promised him the leadership because of his importance as a "minority" leader.[11] He says that he had never agreed to the Janata-Ranga merger, but only to a Janata-Ranga front. Bangarappa feels that by clever manipulation a forward community man has become the chief minister at the cost of a popular minority leader like himself. But this has been contested by Abdul Nazeer Sab, now minister for Rural Development and Panchayati Raj, who argues that Bangarappa went back on his word on the merger of the Janata and Kranti-Ranga.[12] Nazeer Sab an unassuming and committed man was president of the Kranti Ranga. During the leadership crisis Bangarappa would not agree to any name. If his position was that a minority caste person should be selected he could have endorsed the name of Lakshmisagar (a Kumbara—potter) a Janata man from the beginning. But Bangarappa opposed or at least did not consent to any name. Whatever the truth, Bangarappa, a man with a lot of dynamism, lost a lot of goodwill in the process. S.R. Bommai, now minister for industries and commerce; and H.D. Deve Gowda minister for Public Works, were also in the running. Both were with the Janata from the beginning. But Bommai is a Lingayat and Deva Gowda a Vokkaliga—factors which went against them. Bangarappa did not support Nazeer Sab either. In the end Ramakrishna Hegde was chosen as a compromise. It is a pity that a leader with the personality and dynamism of Bangarappa should have denied the state his services by playing his cards badly.

V

The Janata government promises to follow the policies of Devaraj Urs. Personally this is meant to suggest that the interests of the backward classes and minorities are safe. But there are indications that minority caste leaders like Lakshmisagar feel that the major communities dominate the government. Also the fact that Hegde's by-election campaign (Hegde was not an MLA when he was elected leader of the legislative party) was masterminded by Deve Gowda, makes it more difficult for Hegde to exercise any restraint on him. Bommai and Deve Gowda belonging to the two major communities can create problems for Hegde and thus for the minorities.

Further the Hegde government has, among others, a particularly uncomfortable inheritance from the Gundu Rao government. The government order following the Havanur Report was challenged in the Supreme Court. The challenge was inspired by a leader of the Lingayats, M.J.B. Mallardhya a distinguished retired civil servant. The Supreme Court did not pronounce a judgement on the merits of the case but accepted the suggestion of the state government that the latter would constitute another commission to look into the whole issue. As a result the Janata government had to appoint the second KBCC. This second commission has been asked to lay down the criterion for determining backwardness and also undertake an enumeration of the population of different castes in the state. Since nearly ten years have elapsed after a similar exercise was done by the Havanur commission it is doubtful if anything worthwhile can be achieved. Also it is on the cards that the second KBCC will be forced to make some concessions to the Lingayats, currently the most vociferous group demanding the backward tag.

Prior to all this there were signs of the non-Vokkaliga OBCs resenting the presence of the Vokkaligas as a backward community and garnering a major part of the benefits of reservation. There were also moves to bring together the Billavas, Deevaru and Idigas all of whom are traditionally toddy tappers but concentrated respectively in South Kanara, Malnad (Shimoga district) and southern Karnataka and who differ culturally and emotionally (the Deevaru being on the last rung of the ladder) and weave them into a cohesive group. But from 1980 onwards the situation has altered and now the backward classes are groping in the dark.

Notes and References

1. Bangalore, Chikmagalur, Chitradurga, Mandya, Mysore, Shimoga, Tumkur, Hassan, Kolar.
2. Bjorn Hettne, *The Political Economy of Indirect Rule*, London, Curzon Press, 1978.

3. James Manor, *Political Change in our Indian State, Mysore 1917-1955*, Delhi: Manohar, 1977.
4. Castewise population figures are taken from the report of the *Karnataka Backward Classes Commission* (KBCC), 1975 and extrapolated where required.
5. Interview with Devaraj Urs, 4 June 1981.
6. See *Karnataka Backward Classes Commission Report*, Vol. I, 1975.
7. Interview with Devaraj Urs, 4 June 1981.
8. Reported in AIR 1964 S.C. 1823. The petitioners in this case were appealing before the Supreme Court against the judgement of the Mysore High Court in what is popularly known as the Vishwanatha case (AIR 1964 Mys. 132). The majority judgement in the Chitralekha case held that the criteria for ascertaining the social and educational backwardness of a caste "is a complex problem depending upon many circumstances which may vary from State to State". Havanur was of the view that in attempting to interpret the judgement of the Supreme Court in the Balaji case, the Supreme Court gave an incorrect ruling in the Chitralekha case.
9. *Ibid.*
10. James Manor, *Economic and Political Weekly*, Special Number 1980.
11. Interview with Lalitha Natraj, 12 and 13 March, 1983.
12. Interview with Lalitha Natraj, 20 May, 1983.

4

CONGRESS PARTY IN ANDHRA PRADESH
A Review

F.D. VAKIL

THE 1983 assembly elections in Andhra Pradesh have given a new turn to Indian politics. The results have demonstrated that Andhra Pradesh is no more the citadel of the Congress party.

Since the formation of the state in 1956, the Congress had hardly faced any serious challenge. The emergence of a regional party in Telugu Desam and its climb to political power warrant a review of the Congress party's functioning in Andhra Pradesh since independence.

A study of the Congress party's continuation in power for the last 30 years indicates the legitimacy it derived from the landed gentry, agriculture labourers and industrial labourers, and in short, all classes of people. In terms of caste, the party enjoyed allegiance of principal castes in Andhra. The Scheduled Castes, Scheduled Tribes, backward classes and the minorities too supported the Congress. These sections we call 'the support structure' of the Congress. They had reposed faith in the economic and social policies of the Congress like land reforms,

I am grateful to P. Satyanarayan, Deputy Director, Indian Council of Social Science Research (ICSSR), Southern Region, Hyderabad, for providing me the necessary data for this paper.

nationalisation of banks, rural schemes like the Small Farmers Development Agency (SFDA), increase of wages to rural workers and of late, the 20-point programme.

This paper attempts to analyse the decline of the credibility of the Congress in its traditional support groups in Andhra Pradesh because of factionalism, centralised politics, corruption and hunger for power in the party.

The Congress leadership in Andhra area during the freedom movement came essentially from the Brahmins but over the years it gradually shifted to the dominant agricultural castes of Reddys,[1] Kammas and Velmas. As an electoral study puts it, "The party's leadership gradually shifted in the late fifties and early sixties from the urban centres to the rural periphery, from the educated middle class in the cities to the rural elite, from the higher urban based caste to middle peasant castes".[2] The party got the image of a protector of the landed gentry. It could manipulate power through the electoral process. The electoral performance of the Congress after 1956 shows that the masses in Andhra Pradesh did not perceive critically the economic and social policies of the Congress party. They accepted the fact that Congress was the only national party that could deliver the goods. Indira Gandhi assumed the role of saviour of the rural masses.

Now to the crucial question: what went wrong? Why did the voters reject in 1983 a national party in preference to a regional party? The answer could be found in the fact that the last 30 years of mismanagement of the state by the Congress high command had resulted in factionalism, indiscipline and arrogance. To the discredit of the Congress party, it had generated a culture that institutionalised corruption. In the absence of an effective challenge, the one-party dominant system of the Congress party took it for granted that the support structure would remain intact. The Congress party was engaged in developing what could be termed the 'science of mismanagement'. It failed to foresee the consequences of emergence of the market economy which tended to loosen the frozen social structure by creating new alliances and shifting of power structure. In this context, a review of the party in terms of electoral performance, its support structure and an analysis of the unabated factional politics will offer us perhaps the logical explanation to the question "Why did Congress party fail in Andhra Pradesh?"

Shift of support structure—1969 split and after

The electoral performance of the Congress party can be critically examined in terms of shifting of the support structure, particularly after the historic split of Congress in 1969.

"In 1969, the Congress party suffered what appeared to be a major split, disagreement within a large party, especially one covering a wide range of ideological positions in a country of several distinctive regions, were easily understood and had, indeed been a regular feature of the party".[3] Indira Gandhi emerged as a radical spokesman of the down-trodden masses and within the party she asserted herself in playing the power game. The 1969 split had provided the necessary scenario for Indira Gandhi's magnificent win in the 1971 elections. She used her party as an instrument for achieving the social-economic change and, in that process, the party drifted towards identification with the backward classes or weaker section of the party. "The split resulted in the initiation of many radical programmes which sought to transform the Congress party from a party of privileged to a party of masses".[4]

Since 1972, there is a dynamic change of support structure in the Congress party.

The 1972 elections to the fifth assembly elections in Andhra Pradesh was a landmark, for the Congress party became a radical party in the eyes of the common man. In order to restructure the support base of Congress party, Indira Gandhi emphasised the concept of welfarism with the induction of a large number of backward communities. The break-up of the weaker sections is given in Table 4.1.

Keeping this background as a base for an analysis of the fifth assembly, an election survey conducted by the department of political science, Osmania university, gives an interesting insight into the shifting of support structure of the Congress party.

The survey shows that among the various parties, Congress was overwhelmingly favoured; 50.6 per cent of the respondents said that they were close to the Congress party. Class and castewise break-up indicates a wide support to Congress from

TABLE 4.1 : **Backward groups representation in Congress(I) legislature party in 1972**

Name of the section	Nos.
1. Scheduled castes	41
2. Scheduled tribes	11
3. Muslims	18
4. Christians	7
5. Women	32
6. Others	64
Total	173

Source : K.R. Acharya, *The Critical Elections*, Hyderabad, Ramesh Publications, Hyderabad, 1979.

The basic thrust of this move was to change the power structure from the dominant groups to the backward classes. Thus, out of 219 Congress(R) MLAs 173 (81.7%) belonged to the backward groups.

backward classes (58.7%), minorities (43.1%) and the low caste (34.1%). The above study has been able to highlight the overwhelming response of the backward sections to the calculated and deliberate move of the Congress leadership to tilt the power balance in favour of the deprived sections of the society. This self-interested electoral exercise could not have been independent of the ideological compulsions but was a continuation of the 1969 split of the Congress and the first step to build a new power pattern.[5]

TABLE 4.2 : **Castewise distribution of Congress(I) seats, 1978**

Name of the caste	No. of seats
Backward classes	121
Scheduled castes and tribes	49
Muslims	12
Women	4
Christians	3
Reddy	58
Others	42
Total	289

Source: K.R. Acharya, *The Critical Elections*, Hyderabad, Ramesh Publications, 1979.

In the 1978 assembly elections, the selection process of the Congress party candidates followed the 1972 trend of giving a large number of seats to the weaker sections.

The peculiar feature of the Congress(I) was its insistence on caste suffixes, an indication of caste, along with the names of candidates. It was to demonstrate clearly the extent of representation it gave to minorities and weaker sections.[6]

A state-wide study[7] of 1980 parliamentary elections identifies a very large number of Congress(I) supporters. Among those who said that they were close to a particular political party, 70.07 per cent identified with the Congress(I). Among these, 47.5 per cent belonged to the backward classes, 10 per cent to the scheduled castes, and 23.7 per cent to Muslims. This data, when compared to the earlier 1972 elections, reveals a gradual decline of support of backward classes and the minorities. A case study of Medak parliamentary elections significantly shows that among those who were close to the Congress party, 83.3 per cent were Hindus and only 16.6 per cent were Muslims.[8] Castewise analysis shows 50 per cent of Congress(I) supporters as belonging to the backward classes and only 8.3 per cent as belonging to the Scheduled Castes and Scheduled Tribes.

A study of 10 parliamentary constituencies in the 1980 parliamentary elections also confirms the earlier findings that Congress(I) is the only party which derives a large support from different sections, but their support has been declining.[9]

A pre-election survey of the assembly elections in Andhra Pradesh revealed that Congress(I) has 35 per cent support from lower class, 56 per cent from middle class and 10 per cent from high classes.[10] The study showed Telangana as a bastion of Congress(I), accounting for 49 per cent as its supporters. In Andhra region, its support was limited to 30 per cent and in Rayalaseema 22 per cent. The overall percentage of those who identified with a political party is 51 per cent and from this only 27 per cent identified with Congress(I) and 10 per cent with TDP.

Low socio-economic status and Congress(I) support

Studies have confirmed that Congress(I) derives its support

structure from the lower socio-economic status groups. Table 4.3 confirms the above statement.

Data in Table 4.3 shows that Congress(I) does not have support from young voters. A majority of the Congress voters belong to the illiterate section of society. Income-wise, the data shows it is the lower income groups which support the Congress(I) party; caste-wise majority of SCs and BCs had decided to vote for Congress(I). Yadgiri's study of the Medak parliamentary constituency also confirms the fact that the Congress support structure emerges from low socio-economic strata. His study[11] indicates a composition of 72.4 per cent backward classes, 83.9 per cent illiterates and 79.3 per cent of lower income group. In fact the thesis argues that it was a calculated move on the part of the Congress high command to propose Indira Gandhi's candidature for Medak constituency in the 1980 elections. It was based not only upon the low socio-economic conditions of the constituency, but also the low socio-economic status profile of the voters.[12]

Those who had intended to vote for Congress(I) in the 1980 parliamentary elections were asked, "Whom did you vote for in the 1971, 1977 and 1978 elections"? Table 4.4 gives us interesting analysis.

The data shows a considerable rise in the support structure of backward classes and the Scheduled Castes, but as far as the Muslims were concerned, there was a decline of support to Congress(I). The 1983 pre-election study revealed that 18.00 per cent could be called "Congress regulars" [those who voted for Congress(I) in the previous elections and would like to vote for Congress(I) in the 1983 elections] and a large proportion (31.00%) who had voted for Congress(I) in the previous elections were now undecided about their voting choice. It could have been possible for those undecided voters to have caused the swing towards the TDP. About 8.00 per cent of the voters who voted for the Congress(I) in the previous elections decided to vote for other parties. Among these, 6.00 per cent said that they would vote for TDP. The Congress(I) could attract only an insignificant 0.5 per cent among the new voters.

The survey also shows that those who have shifted their loyalties from Congress(I) [who voted in 1978 and 1980 for Congress(I)] to other parties are predominantly from among

TABLE 4.3 : **Voters intention to vote Congress(I)—1980 parliamentary elections**

Age	%	Education	%	Income Rs.	%	Caste	%
21-25 yrs	2.6	Illiterate	68.3	150	52 00	B.C.	63.7(N=215)
26-30 yrs	4.0	Primary	18.3	151-300	24.00	S.C.	55.5(N=108)
		(some Secondary)	8.6	301-500	10.3	Muslims	35.7(N=98)
31-40 yrs	3.3	Secondary	4.0	501-750	7.3		
		Complete		751-1000	4.6		
41-45 yrs	11.00	University	0.6	1000 above	2.00		
46-50 yrs	41.00						
51-60 yrs	18.30						
61 yrs & above	16.33						
Total No. of respondents 750							

Source: Statewide Study of 10 Parliamentary Constituencies, 1980 Parliament elections, Political Science Dept., Osmania University, Hyderabad.

the males, younger age groups, primary and middle school educated urban voters, middle income groups and backward classes. The study also shows that Scheduled Tribes and middle castes voted for opposition parties in 1978 and 1980.

No significant shift of the Congress(I) traditional voter from among females, illiterates, upper castes, low income and rural voters could be discerned.

The overall support structure of Congress(I) can be seen from Table 4.5.

TABLE 4.4 : **Backward class, Scheduled Castes, Muslim voters of Congress(I)—1971, 1977 and 1979**

	1971 Lok Sabha Voted %	1977 Lok Sabha Voted %	1979 Assembly election %
B.C.	57.67	72.09	72.55
S.C.	56.48	67.59	67.59
Muslims	20.40	36.73	27.55

Source: Statewide study of 10 Parliamentary Constituencies, 1980 Parliament elections. Political Science Dept., Osmania University Hyderabad.

Data in Table 4.6 also shows a significant decline in the backward class and Muslim support. In fact the subsequent performance of the Congress(I) in 1983 elections proved that the backward classes played a decisive role in shifting of support structure from Congress to TDP.

Harijans and Muslims constitute up to 30 per cent of the electorate in A.P. The 1983 results showed that their support to Congress(I) could no more be taken for granted because of two reasons: (a) these sections do not vote on the basis of caste or religion any longer, and (b) they do not see Congress(I) as the protector of their interests. While in 1978 the Congress(I) had won over three-fourths of all SC seats, in 1983 it conceded 68 per cent of them to TDP (see Table 4.7). In constituencies where the Harijan population is significantly higher, TDP won absolute majority surpassing the 1978 Congress(I) record. In short the support Congress(I) received from the reserved

TABLE 4.5 : **Congress(I) support structure—1983 election study**

Age	%	Sex	%	Education	%	Occupation	%	Income	%	R/U	%
Yrs 21-35	36.00	M	61.00	Illiterates	55.00	Labourer	17.00	Low income	68.00	Urban	27.00
				Primary	27.00	Household	15.00			Rural	73.00
36-50	39.00	F	39.00	Middle	14.00	White-collared	5.00				
				College	4.00	Unskilled	12.00				
						Business	6.00				
Total No. of respondents 886											

Source: Pre-election Survey of A.P. assembly elections 1983, Political Science Dept., Osmania University, Hyderabad.

constituencies proved the lowest level, thus eroding its traditional support group base.

TABLE 4.6 : **Congress(I) support structure—1983 election study—Socio-Economic Status (SES), Castewise***

SES	%	Caste	%	Minorities	%
Higher	10.00	SC/ST	26.00	Muslim	17.00
Middle	56.00	B.C.	38.00		
Low	35.00	Middle	12.00		
		Upper	5.00		
Total No. of respondents 800					

*A cumulative index of socio-economic status based on caste education and income indicates the support structure of political parties among the various classes in society.

Source: Pre-election survey of A.P. Assembly elections, 1983, Political Science Dept., Osmania University, Hyderabad.

TABLE 4.7 : **Andhra Pradesh reserved constituency—Congress(I) position, 1983**

Region	SC seats	ST seats	Total	Seats won by Congress(I)
Andhra	16	7	23	2
Rayalaseema	7	—	7	1
Telangana	15	6	21	11
Total	38	13	51	14

Source: Data A.P. 1983, Data News Features, Hyderabad, 1983.

In at least 30 constituencies where Muslims form the majority, Congress(I) fared badly securing less than a quarter of the total vote. In four-fifths of them it had to face stiff opposition from rival Muslim candidates, some of them supported by Majlis Ittehadul Musulmeen. Even in popular votes the percentage shows the decline of Congress(I) support base (see Tables 4.16 and 4.17).

TABLE 4.8 : **First general election in Hyderabad State, 1952—Comparative voting pattern in Hyderabad and Telangana area**

Name of the Party	Hyderabad state			Telangana area*		
	Seats contested	Seats won	Votes polled %	Seats contested	Seats won	Votes polled %
Congress	173	91+2**	41.40	98	44	38.17
Socialist	57	11	13.75	58	11	13.74
People Democratic Party***	78	42	21.40	45	36	26.12
Kisan Mazdoor Praja Party Ram Rajya Parishad S.C. Federation Party Republican Party Depressed Class Association United S.C. Federation Independents League	152	29	23.45	123	7	21.79
Total	460	175	100.C0	324	98	100.00

*On the eve of the first general elections, 1952, Hyderabad state consisted of four Subhas (units for administrative convenience) and 17 districts. Telangana area had 9 districts: Warangal, Adilabad, Kareemnagar, Medak, Nizamabad, Nalgunda, Mahboobnagar, Atraf Balda and Bhagat. The other two linguistic regions were: Marathwada (Aurangabad, Bhir, Osmanabad, Paıbhani, Nanded), Karnataka (Gulbarga, Raichur, Bidar).

**Congress Party won 2 seats uncontested.

***The Communist Party, which was banned, fought the elections under PDF label.

Source: Report on the First General Election in India: 1951-52, Vol. I & II, Election Commission of India, 1953.

II

ELECTORAL PERFORMANCE AND FACTIONALISM

There was an unquestioned dominance of the Congress party in the state from the first general election and in the subsequent elections the Congress party secured a comfortable majority. In this section we shall look briefly into the factional politics which destroyed the Congress dominance.

In the first general election in Hyderabad state as many as 10 political parties contested but the Congress emerged as the largest single party. (See Table 4.8)

Similarly in Telugu speaking areas of Madras the parties represented were Congress, Communist, Forward Boc (Marxist), Socialist Party, Kisan Mazdoor Praja Party, Ram Rajya Parishad, Hindu Mahasabha, Muslim League, Scheduled Castes Federation and Krishikar Lok Party.

TABLE 4.9 : **First general elections to Andhra area (Madras State)—1951-52**

Name of the Party	Seats contested	Seats won	Votes polled %
Congress	133	40	30.78
Socialist	50	6	6.10
Communist	63	41	16.45
Others (KLP, KMPP, Forward Bloc, Hind Mazdoor Sabha, Ram Rajya Parishad, SCF, ML)	161	37	23.02
Independents	221	17	23.25
Total	628	141	

Source: *Elections in India, State Legislatures Since 1952*, Shivlal, Election Archives, Institute for Electoral Studies, New Delhi.

Table 4.9 shows that Congress could secure 93 seats polling 41.40 per cent of votes. In the Telangana region the Congress party secured 44 seats polling 38.17 per cent of the votes.

The Andhra counterpart of Madras state witnessed a fall in the Congress. The party contested 133 seats and secured 40, polling 30.78 per cent votes (see Table 4.9). The fall of the Congress image may be attributed generally to the infighting, mutual bickerings and political dissensions among its leaders.[13]

The Congress factionalism was mainly responsible for the leaders like Ranga and Prakasam to leave the party and organise separate political forums.[14]

1955—Mid-term poll

When the United Front ministry of Prakasam resigned following a vote of no-confidence, Andhra Pradesh faced a mid-term poll in 1955.

The Congress decided to face the elections as a United Front of Congress, KLP and Praja Party in view of facing a stiff opposition from the Communists whose strength in the last Assembly was 41 out of 140 seats.

As seen from Table 4.10, the Congress contested 142 and secured 118 seats with 43.40 per cent votes. The result gave the necessary fillip to the Congress party to contain the communal influence and bring political stability.

TABLE 4.10 : **General elections in Andhra (1955)**

Name of the Party	Seats contested	Seats won	Votes polled %
Indian National Congress	139	116+3*	39.35
Praja Socialist Party	45	13	5.58
Communist Party of India	169	15	31.13
All India Bharatiya Jan Sangh	6	—	0.10
Krishikar Lok Party	37	22	7.26
Praja Party	12	5	2.79
Others (Independents)	170	22	13.78
Total	578	196	

*Three were returned uncontested.

Source: *Report on the General Election to the Andhra Legislative Assembly 1955*, Election Commission, New Delhi, 1956, pp. 30-31.

B. Gopal Reddy assumed the reigns of the government which heralded the entry of the dominant Reddy caste in Andhra politics.

1956—Party position

Following the recommendations of the States Reorganisation Commission, when the linguistic states were created in India, the enlarged state of Andhra Pradesh came into existence on 1 November, 1956. Then the Congress had 163 seats out of 297 in the Andhra Pradesh legislature.

TABLE 4.11 : **Party position in the legislature when Andhra Pradesh came into existence**

Party	Seats
Congress	163
PSP & Socialist	24
Communist	51
Scheduled Caste Federation (SCF)	3
Krishikar Lok Paksh (KLP)	22
Praja Party	5
Independents	29
Total	297

Source : G. Ram Reddy, B.A.V. Sharma (Eds.), *State Government and Politics: Andhra Pradesh*, Sterling, New Delhi, 1979.

The Congress party in view of the majority in the state assembly formed the government under the leadership of Neelam Sanjeeva Reddy. This was the only occasion where the Congress Legislature Party in Andhra Pradesh was given the liberty of electing its leader democratically.[15] While the Congress began to take roots because of stability, it also saw the beginning of factionalism. In fact, the election of Sanjeeva Reddy divided the Congress in the state into two groups leading to factionalism and ultimately several Congressmen resigned to form a new party, called the Socialist Democratic Party.

The 1957 elections

In the General Elections of 1957, elections to the legislative assembly were held only in the Telangana region. On the recommendations of the States Reorganisation Commission the term of the Andhra members was extended to seven years to coincide with the Third General Elections in 1962. Therefore elections for Andhra region were not held for the 196 seats during 1957.

TABLE 4.12 : **Second general elections in Telangana, 1957**

Name of the Party	Seats contested	Seats won	Percentage of votes polled
Congress	105	70	47.30
Jan Sangh	2	—	0.16
PSP (Socialist & Kisan Mazdoor Praja Party)	27	1	5.30
Communist	65	20	26.10
Scheduled Caste Federation	2	1	0.60
Peasants and Workers Party	7	—	1.70
Praja Party	7	1	0.80
United Scheduled Caste Federation (USCF)	2	—	NA
Independents	83	12	18 00
Total	300	105	100.00

Source: G. Ram Reddy, B.A.V. Sharma (Eds.), *State Government and Politics*: *Andhra Pradesh*, Sterling, New Delhi, 1979.

The Congress party contested all the 105 seats and secured 70 seats. polling 47.30 per cent votes. Congress made considerable improvement in terms of seats as well as popular votes. The polling trend indicated a considerable swing towards Congress.

Emergence of dissidents within Congress

Following the elections, Chenna Reddy, a dissident leader, demanded the election of a new leader. The Congress high command conceded to the request for re-election of the leader. Dissidents withdrew finding no support. Subsequently Sanjeeva Reddy was elected leader. Meanwhile the partners of the United Front of Andhra, namely, KLP with 22 MLAs, Praja Party with 5 MLAs and 2 Independents merged with the Congress and the party position of Congress after 1957 rose to 216 (break-up: Andhra Congress 119, Telangana Congress 68, KLP 22, Praja Party 5, Independents 2).

Thus the strength of the Congress party in the Assembly became unassailable. But by 1958, intense factionalism emerged within the party.

Evidently, one of the reasons for factionalism in the Congress from 1952 till 1962 was the pluralistic character of the party.[16] The party had an ability to hold different sections of society in its fold.

"The Congress party has a more heterogeneous and differentiated social, economic and demographic support base than any other party. It is not only in terms of its special hold over all regions but also in terms of its ability to cut across the various divisions of castes, occupation, economic class and demographic differentiations, even though it may draw a little more support from certain segments and a little less from certain others—on the whole all the social, economic, ethnic categories are almost evenly represented amongst its supporters".[17] But this ability declined to become a liability.

The formation in 1957 of Andhra Pradesh Congress Committee and the Hyderabad Congress Committee encouraged the growth of factionalism. The Congressmen of Telangana could not work in unity with their counterparts in the Andhra region, obviously because of regional diversity. The Congress was a house divided because of regional and sub-regional rivalry. For instance, the Hyderabad Pradesh Congress Committee was ridden with factional groups led by Swami Ramananda Tirtha, Ramakrishna Rao and the K.V. Ranga Reddy factions. Similarly, the Andhra Congress had Pattabhi group, Prakasam group, Gopal Reddy group and Sanjeeva Reddy group.

Caste factor

Following the merger of former partners of the United Front, (KLP and Praja in the Congress) and the formation of the enlarged Andhra Pradesh Congress Committee, the rivalry between Reddys and Kammas came to an end. Interestingly, in its place intra-caste rivalry on a horizontal plane among the Reddys of Telangana and Andhra soon surfaced.[18]

Sanjeeva Reddy wanted to make Brahmananda Reddy the leader of Congress Legislature Party. The contenders for leadership were Alluri Satyanarayan Raju from Circars and

K.V. Ranga Reddy from Telangana. Finally, the leadership fell on Sanjeeviah. As a result, 1960-62 witnessed a vertical clash on the caste lines: Reddys on one hand and scheduled castes and backward classes on the other. Factional politics intensified. A powerful group emerged within the legislature party known as United Front. Brahmananda Reddy and A.C. Subba Reddy led the Front. Obviously, this factional politics betrayed caste rivalries. A signature campaign was launched for a change in the leadership. Though Nehru put down the activities of the Front, one could see the spill-over of the caste rivalries during the 1962 elections where the Congress candidates were defeated by the leaders of local bodies.

In the selection of Congress candidates for 1962 elections Sanjeeva Reddy played a decisive role. The 1962 election results revealed factional politics plaguing the party. From 216 seats in the previous assembly, they had to be content with 177 and 39 seats were lost to others.

TABLE 4.13 : **Third general elections in 1962**

Name of the party	Seats contested	Seats won	Votes polled %
Congress	294	177	47.25
Swatantra	141	19	10.40
Jan Sangh	70	—	1.04
PSP	6	—	0.52
Socialist	15	2	0.62
Communist	136	51	19.63
R.P.I.	18	—	0.42
Majlis and others	1	1	0.09
Independents	301	50	20.03
Total	982	300	100.00

Source : *Elections in India, State Legislatures since 1952*, Shivlal, Election Archives, Institute for Electoral Studies, New Delhi.

The Congress party contested 294 seats and won 177, polling 47.25 per cent popular votes. The success of Independents was mainly due to Congress factional politics. Among the 50

Independents, 30 were rebel Congressmen. The rebel Congressmen were followers of Sanjeeva Reddy and they formed a United Democratic Front (UDF) in the legislature and later joined the Congress in February 1965. Following the 1962 elections, Sanjeeva Reddy staged a come-back and assumed leadership of the state legislature party. The Sanjeeva Reddy ministry lasted till 1964. He had to resign on the adverse verdict of the Supreme Court in the Kurnool Transport Nationalisation case.[19]

The exit of Sanjeeva Reddy saw the entry of Brahmananda Reddy. He extended political patronage to those who opposed Sanjeeva Reddy. It was a strategic move to strengthen his roots. He even allowed the National Democratic Front of K.V. Reddy to merge with Congress. These actions of the chief minister created a sharp cleavage within the Congress ranks which ultimately divided the Congress into "Officials and Dissidents", the former supporting the chief minister and the latter supporting Sanjeeva Reddy.[20]

During that period, the factional fights produced two powerful agitations: one, for the autonomy of Osmania University and the second for a steel plant in Andhra Pradesh. The former agitation was directed against the ministerialists and the latter against Sanjeeva Reddy.

The factional fight split the cabinet. A.C. Subba Reddy with the support of half of his ministerial colleagues revolted against Brahmananda Reddy. The fight was for the control of the party organisation.

The factional politics of the Congress party entered the 1964 panchayat elections when out of 20 Zilla Parishads, 14 were captured by the ministerialist group. It also crept into the Indian National Trade Union Congress and student groups. The party's interest as well as the state's interests were relegated to the background with the in-fighting. Fragmentation of the Congress party at this stage was because of a clash of personalities between Brahmananda Reddy and Sanjeeva Reddy.

1967 elections

The selection of Congress candidates in the 1967 elections showed a majority of candidates belonging to the ministerialists. Meanwhile a rival list was prepared by the dissidents. A formula was devised bv the central election committee whereby the ministerialists enjoyed a majority of 40.

As seen from Table 4.14, there was a decline in the seats and popular votes. The results clearly reflected not only the growing strength of the rival factions in the Congress but also their strength among the 'Congress' Independents. These Independents formed a group known as Peoples Democratic Party (PDP). Later they merged with the Congress raising the Congress strength to 200. In the process Brahmananda Reddy emerged very powerful.

TABLE 4.14 : **Fourth general elections—1967—Pattern of voting**

Name of the party	Seats contested	Seats won	Votes polled %
Congress	285	165	45.32
Swatantra	89	29	9.84
Jan Sangh	80	3	2.11
SSP	9	1	0.36
CPI	103	10	7.78
CPI(M)	82	9	7.61
PSP	2	—	0.21
RPI	11	2	0.27
Majlis	7	3	0.53
Praja Party	1	1	NA
Independents	395	64	25.98
Total	1064	287	100.00

Source : *Elections in India, State Legislatures since 1952*, Shivlal, Election Archives, Institute for Electoral Studies, New Delhi.

In Brahmananda Reddy's cabinet only one dissident leader was included. Chenna Reddy who had earlier supported Brahmananda Reddy in 1966 was given the cabinet No. 2 post. This created considerable resentment among the ministers. A factional group within the cabinet was responsible for sending Chenna Reddy to the centre.

Meanwhile the death of A.C. Reddy saw the dissidents lying low. Thcy were anxiously waiting for an opportune time. The Telangana agitation during 1969 came handy to the dissidents whose only plan was to dislodge the Chief Minister.

A sizeable number of Telangana Congress legislators (29) formed themselves into United Front which functioned as the main opposition in state legislative assembly. After the exit of Brahmananda Reddy, the United Front merged with Congress. The exit of Brahmananda Reddy indicated how factional politics in the Congress party could remove a powerful leader who not only enjoyed the support of Congress legislators but also of Zilla Parishad chairmen.

The seventh Congress ministry since 1956 came into the offing with factional politics. This time, the Telangana Praja Samithi emerged in opposition to the Congress. Factional politics were accentuated to such an extent that, though Brahmananda Reddy was responsible for installing P.V. Narasimha Rao as chief minister, his own men were excluded from Rao's cabinet. Factions emerged within the TPS ranks when Manik Rao parted company with Chenna Reddy.

The direct interference by central leaders had antagonised the factional groups. Once again the interest of the state was relegated to the background when a violent Andhra agitation erupted. The level to which the Congress party was reduced in the process of factional politics could be seen in P.V. Narasimha Rao's public statement: "I have become the chief minister by a stroke of luck and not by adopting crooked means or by influencing the members and forming groups in the Congress(R) party".[21] P.V. Narasimha Rao's style of functioning and his total dependence on Delhi in decision-making not only lowered the image of the party, but also his own. He was confronted with a hostile legislature party. Removing powers of the Zilla Parishads further alienated him. The dominant caste groups were not appreciative of the fact that he, being a Brahmin, initiated a policy of giving greater representation to backward classes and the weaker sections in the legislature and the council of ministers.

Prior to the 1972 elections, the Congress high command decided to replace the Pradesh Congress Committee by *ad hoc* Pradesh Congress Committees. This unusual and hasty act of the party high command raised suspicions that the prime minister planned to have Pradesh committees of her choice in an attempt to gain total control over state units. After hectic pressures from the different regions, a new *ad hoc* Congress committee of 95 members headed by Md. Ismail, a Congress MLA from the Andhra region was formed. Brahmananda Reddy was excluded. It was decided that representation of weaker sections should be to the extent of 60 per cent (women 40 seats, minorities 12 seats). Meanwhile the selection process led to considerable dissatisfaction, resulting in 1735 nominations being filed in the first instance, of which 300 were nominations by rebel Congressmen.

The *ad hoc* committee had a list of 1400 Congressmen charged with working against Congress nominees.

TABLE 4.15 : **Voting pattern in the fifth A.P. assembly elections 1972**

Name of the party	Seats contested	Seats won	Votes polled %
Indian National Congress	287	219	52.29
Bhartiya Jan Sangh	56	—	1.86
Communist Party of India	59	7	5.98
CPI (M)	32	1	3.18
Swatantra	20	2	1.98
Indian National Congress (O)	11	—	0.32
Socialist Party	4	—	0.07
Independents	488	57	32.22
Others*	56	1	2.11
Total	1013	287	100.00

*D.M.K., Republican Party of India (Khobrogade); Minorities League, Sampurna Telangana Praja Samithi, Backward Classes Mahasabha.

Source : *Report on the General Elections to the Legislative Assemblies of India (1970-72)*, Vol. II, pp 111-115, Election Commission of India 1976.

Immediately after the poll of 1972, some Telangana leaders and other leaders like Brahmananda Reddy and Raghunath Reddy wanted to remove P.V. Narasimha Rao. The policy of the high command was not to disturb the leadership. When alienated by the dominant caste, Rao tried to create his own support structure by forging links with Harijans, backward classes and minorities. The Congress party thus set the process of polarisation of Andhra Pradesh politics along caste and class lines. This resulted in an agitation for a separate Andhra state in 1972.[22]

P.V. Narasimha Rao resigned. Once again the party succeeded in removing a chief minister who could not survive factionalism. Thc abject surrender to the central leadership was demonstrated when on 1 December 1973 the Congress legislature party met and passed a unanimous resolution, reaffirming faith in the leadership of Indira Gandhi. The resolution read: "The leader so chosen by prime minister will be deemed to have been elected by the party at this meeting."[23] Interestingly, the resolution was moved by P.V. Narasimha Rao.

Meanwhile, the Andhra agitation created a new dimension in the factional politics. Congressmen belonging to the former TPS became staunch integrationists and the former integrationists became separatists.

The extent to which the Congress leaders indulged in the power game could be seen when P.V. Narasimha Rao and Brahmananda Reddy launched a signature campaign to thwart Vengal Rao's nomination to the leadership of the legislature, though they could not suggest any alternative. The advent of Vengal Rao saw a major setback to the Brahmananda Reddy group. Some of Brahmananda Reddy's followers joined Vengal Rao.

1977 elections and regrouping of factions

The 1977 elections saw the fall of the Congress ministry at the centre. This resulted in a new type of factionalism in Andhra Pradesh. Brahmananda Reddy's candidature for the Congress party presidentship was rejected by Vengal Rao. He even threatened to resign. Meanwhile Anjaiah and Rajaram, who were loyal to P.V. Narasimha Rao, formed an effective faction resulting in Vengal Rao joining Brahmananda Reddy's group. The cabinet was expanded to accommodate Brahmananda Reddy's men. Brahmananda Reddy's creation of a new ad hoc body for the state Congress was resented by the dissident group with the former ministerialists becoming dissident and former dissidents becoming ministerialists. It ultimately led to the Congress split. K. Rajamallu, T. Anjaiah and Dharma Reddy resigned from the cabinet in December, 1977. Later they formed Congress(I) under the leadership of Chenna Reddy.

The emergence of the Janata at the centre and the split in the Congress party had an impact on state politics. The Congress party in the state was divided in 1978 and the official unit of Congress(I) came into existence on 18 January 1978.

In the 1978 elections the Congress led by Brahmananda Reddy and Janata entered into electoral adjustments with CPI and CPI (M) respectively. The Congress (I) was the only party which contested without any alliance. The Congress (Reddy) contested 257 seats and won only 30 seats. The Congress(I) contested 290 seats and won 175 seats with 39.24 per cent of the votes polled. Congress(I), though free from rebels, was handicapped with deep divisions in the party ranks. Divisions emerged between supporters of Chenna Reddy and P.V. Narasimha Rao and C. Rajaram groups.

Once again the Congress(I) exposed the usual factional fights when the question of electing a leader arose. Chenna Reddy and G. Rajaram staked their claim. After hectic bargaining, G. Rajaram withdrew in favour of Chenna Reddy. What Rajni Kothari had said of Congress was true: "Congress system has always been a system of coalition, multi-group in character, and informed by a continuous process of internal bargaining and mobility."[4] Even though the party returned with absolute majority, differences broke out. A dissident group was formed within the organisation of the party questioning Chenna Reddy's continuance as president of Congress(I).

1978-83—sharpening of Congress(I) dissidence

This was a period when the high command played havoc with the state politics. The majority legislature party was not allowed to make decisions.

This period was very crucial and significant in the context of the future political change in the state. The party succeeded in creating an image where personal interests of the Congress(I) leader were more important than the party, leave alone the interest of the state as such. Chenna Reddy's tenure brought to the surface three types of groups within the Congress (I); (1) the Chenna Reddy group, (2) the Anti-Andhra separatist group consisting of P.V. Narasimha Rao, and (3) the weaker sections. To sustain the political power, they had to be manipulated and each chief minister in the state had his own style of doing it. In order to neutralize the pulls and strains of the different groups and factions, Chenna Reddy included six members in his cabinet from outside. He encouraged defections. In two and a half years, 30 Congress(U) members were reduced to 3, and 60 Janata to 16. Even the only CPI(ML) was admitted into Congress(I). From the council he won over his critic K. Rosaiah, who was given a berth in the cabinet. Elevation of N. Bhaskar Rao to the cabinet minister level created ill-will among other senior ministers.

The emergence of dissidents within the cabinet came to the surface when N. Bhaskar Rao moved closer to Sanjay Gandhi. Chenna Reddy saw this as a threat and immediately used his prerogative in changing Rao's earlier protfolio to an insignificant one. Dissident Congress leaders, ministers and legislators rallied around Bhaskar Rao. Six ministers were removed by Reddy and one resigned. The new political situation in fact injected a new formidable force into the ranks of the dissidents. Meanwhile his style of functioning coupled with the pompous celebration of his 60th birthday led to 16 of his ministers seeking Indira Gandhi's permission to resign. Factional feuds resulted in the total stoppage of administration and many legislators turned rebels. Communication between the dissident ministers and the chief minister broke down. Fifteen ministers belonging to the dissident group camped in Delhi for the removal of Reddy. Finally, on 10 October 1980, Chenna Reddy resigned. Once again the Congress(I) leaders relegated the interests of the state to a secondary position in their personal pursuit of power.

Loyalty factor

The exit of Chenna Reddy brought to surface the Congress(I) legislators' lack of power to assert themselves. The Congress(I) leaders of the state allowed Indira Gandhi to use her clout in imposing a leader. The total subjugation of the state Congress(I) to the central leadership could be gauged, when a defeated candidate in the assembly elections from Musheerabad constituency and a member of the Rajya Sabha (himself a state dissident leader), Anjaiah was made the leader. Apart from other arguments, Anjaiah's defeat in Musheerabad should have been enough for his elimination but the Congress ethos made him the chief minister. Of course Anjaiah's loyalty to Indira Gandhi mattered more than anything else.

At this stage, the Congress(I) lowered its image to the point of ridicule. Making and expanding the ministry was done in Delhi. It was a 61 member ministry. Anjaiah accommodated representatives of all the factions. The large sized ministry provided conducive grounds for the emergence of a dissident group within three months. All the ministers in the state were asked to resign on 13 January 1981.

The style of functioning of Anjaiah supplemented by active factionalism among the party men created a feeling of disgust among the people. The elections held in Andhra Pradesh during this period were a clear indicator of things to come. In the elections to the upper house, the Congress(I) lost as many as 9 seats out of 30. The party fared badly in the Corporation elections held in Vijayawada and Vishakhapatnam. Congress(I)'s credibility to deliver an honest administration was doubted by people. Charges of corruption and favouritism were levelled by the rivals within the party. Anjaiah had ittle time for administration, for he was busy pruning or expanding his cabinet. Every third Congress(I) MLA in Andhra Pradesh became a minister.

Meanwhile the high command wanted Anjaiah to prune his cabinet. He dropped 16 ministers, prominent among them were Sanjeeva Reddy's son-in-law, C. Rambhupal Reddy, K.V. Krishna Reddy (Brahmananda Reddy's nephew), and Sreenivasulu Reddy.

The first major challenge to Anjaiah came from N. Bhaskar Rao whom Anjaiah later sacked. Dissidents along with Bhaskara Rao moved to Delhi with the one-point programme of "removal of Anjaiah". The high command was convinced that Anjaiah was hardly the person who could lead the party to victory in the ensuing assembly elections. The central leadership "discovered" that he lacked political depth and shrewdness and they wanted a leader who could command respect of the administration and help selection of candidates. The AICC(I) general secretary, Shyam Sunder Mahapatra, was sent to Hyderabad to assess the situation.

It was decided to remove M.A. Aziz, the APCC(I) president. Anjaiah wanted to nominate E. Krishna Murthy, a former minister to the post of APCC(I) president. The high command overruled the chief minister by nominating Kona Prabhakar Rao, a follower of P.V. Narasimha Rao.

The emergence of a reconstituted party organisation saw shifting of the power centre. Kona Prabhakar suspended among others two members of Anjaiah's cabinet, C. Das and Chandrababu Naidu, for violating party discipline. The suspension was made without consulting the chief minister.

The president of APCC(I) and the chief minister were working on parallel lines, and once again a chief minister who had absolute majority in the assembly was unceremoniously removed from office.

B. Venkatram Reddy was chosen chief minister after a close race between Kona Prabhakar Rao, N. Janardhan Reddy and Baga Reddy. Venkatram Reddy was a non-starter. Congress(I) unity and discipline were needed during the Rajya Sabha elections. Though Congress(I) had the requisite strength to elect all the six members from the state, the state leadership was not prepared to field six candidates. It decided to field only 5 nominees, for the party leaders could foresee large-scale cross-voting.

The elections set an all-time record in cross-voting by the Congress(I) MLAs. The Janata party candidate Babul Reddy was declared elected on the first count. Shockingly, no Congress(I) nominee was selected on the first count. About 60 Congress(I) members indulged in cross-voting. Meanwhile the emergence of Telugu Desam and the growing popularity of N.T. Rama Rao saw the exit of yet another chief minister. Venkatram Reddy was replaced by K. Vijayabhaskar Reddy in September 1982. This change signalled an early poll. There was an element of lack of political skill and maturity in the high command's decision to bring in Vijayabhaskar Reddy from the Lok Sabha and impose him upon the Congress(I) legislature party. Succumbing to the pressures of the dissidents, the chief minister was asked to expand the ministry. With the former minister's legacy of factional politics which was revived by Venkatram Reddy and Anjaiah, many managed to gate-crash into the cabinet. Ministers who were suspected of wide-scale corruption were also accommodated. M. Baga Reddy who was involved in the cement scandal was a case in point. The very purpose of inducting Vijayabhaskar Reddy from Lok Sabha to revitalize the ageing party was brought to naught by not allowing him to function independently.

Pre-1983 election scene

Since the Congress splits in 1969 and 1977, the infighting in the party had never been so acute as it was just before the 1983 elections. Added to that, the party had institutionalised corruption.[25] This was all the more manifest in the election campaign of the Congress(I). For instance, more than 1000 Congress(I) jeeps criss-crossed the entire state during this period.[26] In this context the electorate had to opt for *status quo* or change. Telugu Desam decided to contest 287 seats along with Maneka's Sanjay Vichar Manch (5 seats). About 50 ex-Congressmen were in the ranks of Telugu Desam. The lack of confidence on the part of the high command towards the state leadership was evident during the campaign. Poll observers from northern India were posted. Sixty Congress (I) legislators and leaders from U.P. and Haryana camped in Karimnagar district alone.

The caste-wise data of contestants shows that the Congress high command deviated from the earlier 1972 and 1978 assembly elections. Then the weaker sections were allotted nearly 60 per cent of seats but in 1983 the party allotted only 30 per cent of seats to the weaker sections.[27]

TABLE 4.16 : **Andhra Pradesh—1983 assembly elections—Details of the election results**

Name of party	Contested	Elected	Forfeited deposit	Votes polled	%
A. National parties					
Indian National Congress	294	60	13	7,087,318	33.56
Indian Congress (Socialist)	9	—	7	44,288	0.21
Janata Party	44	1	39	204,170	0.97
Lok Dal	33	—	26	193,880	0.92
Communist Party of India	48	4	29	588,144	2.78
Communist Party of India (Marxist)	28	5	14	425,109	2.01
Bhartiya Janata Party	80	3	62	582,464	2.76
B. State parties					
Indian Congress(J)*	86	1	85	119,372	0.57
C. Independents and others					
Telugu Desam	293	203	29	9,821,972	46.51
Independents	805	17	752	2,050,395	9.71
Total	1,720	294	1,056	21,117.112	100.00

*State Party in Haryana.

Source: Election Commission of India. *Report on the Election to the office of President of India, 1982 and Legislative Assemblies, Delhi Metropolitan Council, 1982-83*, New Delhi, 1983, p. 78.

There was a powerful swing in favour of Telugu Desam. The party's impact, particularly on the coastal belt from Nellore district to Srikakulam district, which comprised 134 constituencies was spectacular. Here the TDP bagged 119 seats out of 134, Congress(I) bagged 9, BJP 1, CPI and Congress rebels 4. In the Rayalaseema district, village factionalism and Congress(I) in-fighting helped the Telugu Desam. In the Telangana region TDP and Congress (I) bagged 43 seats each.

TABLE 4.17 : Region-wise Congress(I) performance—1978 and 1983 elections

Region	Total seats	votes polled % 1978	votes polled % 1983	Seats won 1978	Seats won 1983
Andhra	134	37.1	30.80	75	10
Rayalaseema	53	40.7	35.42	36	7
Telangana	107	38.6	36.26	64	43
Total	294	38.3	33.56	175	60

Source: *Data Andhra Pradesh 1983*, Data News Features, Hyderabad 1983.

Table 4.17 indicates the downward slide in Congress(I) performance as compared to 1978 assembly elections.

The performance of Congress(I) in 1983 in the reserved constituencies, when analysed in the context of our earlier data regarding the support structure of Congress(I), shows poor performance. The reserved constituency offers the necessary socio-economic base for the ruling party to derive necessary support from the socially, economically and educationally backward voters.

CONCLUSION

The fundamental political culture of Congress apart from the earlier factionalism within party, has been Indira Gandhi's charisma and subsequently her authoritarianism. The 1972 assembly elections reflected her charismatic power. The 1969 split of the Congress partly provided the necessary background to project her party as champion of the down-trodden masses. The attempt made by the Congress party in the state for structural changes in the agrarian structure through the legislative Acts of Land Reforms (1972) consolidated the support of the Congress party among the weaker sections. In this process, the party could secure 52.29 per cent of the popular votes. The popularity of Indira Gandhi after the party split in 1969, instead of stabilising the party, had a negative impact on the growth of the party system. She did play the role of vote catcher but along with it a process of de-institutionalisation was initiated which relegated the Congress party organisation to a position of no consequence. In real terms, a Congress(I) vote was in fact a vote for Indira Gandhi. In the process the Congress(I) functioned on a seemingly inflated feeling of stability. In this context we may take note of the fact of a highly exaggerated membership drive of Congress(I) by inducting bogus membership all these years.

The 1977 Lok Sabha and the 1972 assembly election results showed the voters' preference for Indira Gandhi in terms of promises and performance. The 57.83 per cent of popular votes gained by Congress(I) in 1977 Lok Sabha elections reflected the performance factor. The state of Andhra Pradesh benefited from the economic implementation of programmes during the emergency period. The effective role of the over-zealous chief minister and bureaucrats in initiating the 20-point programme further widened the Congress(I) support base. In fact, Indira Gandhi's 20-point programme could compensate the no-performance of the land reforms measures.

The actual decline of popular support of the party was evident from the data of 1978 assembly elections. The loss of considerable votes could be attributed to the fact that Congress party could not live up to the expectation of a government that performs but it was content to play the role of a government that promises.

The earlier small benefits which the rural masses could get from the 20-point programmes over a period became a liability. The fact was that because of bureaucratic and political irritants, sustenance of economic benefits proved to be costlier than the actual benefits that accrued from the 20-point programme.

The 1983 election saw the reassertion of accountability as seen during the 1967 election. The 1983 political situation was also an outcome of the cumulative effects of factional politics which lowered the national character of the party to merely an organisation where men joined to achieve their ends and use the said organisation like a business venture.

Besides the above factors, the most telling impact on the

party has been the personalised approach to politics of Indira Gandhi, the party evolved a political culture reflecting Indira Gandhi's authoritarianism. She did not allow leaders with grassroots bases to grow, nor men of dynamic character to rise. In her calculations, it appears that Chenna Reddy can be more dangerous than N.T. Rama Rao of Telugu Desam Party. This explains the fact that no Congress chief minister in Andhra Pradesh continued in office for a period coterminous with that of the legislative assembly.

The party in order to revitalise itself must undergo a catharsis in order to get rid of the elements that have been responsible for its pathetic performance.

All is not lost for Congress(I) as a party that can come back to power. One should not forget the fact that the party secured 33.56 per cent of popular votes in the 1983 election. With an improvement of 6 to 9 per cent in popular votes it could again return to power.

Notes and References

1. The 1955 mid-term elections in the state heralded the entry of the dominant Reddy caste.
2. B.A.V. Sharma and K Madhusudhan Reddy, Electoral politics and voting behaviour, in G. Ram Reddy and B.A.V. Sharma (Ed.), *State Government and Politics*, Sterling, New Delhi, 1979, p. 469.
3. Biplab Dasgupta, W.H. Morris Jones, *Patterns and Trends in Indian Politics: An Ecological Analysis of Aggregate Data on Society and Elections*, Allied Publishers, Bombay, 1975, pp. 15-16.
4. B.A.V. Sharma, Caste, class and voting behaviour, *Mimeographed.*
5. G. Ram Reddy, "Summary of the report on the fifth assembly election in Andhra Pradesh: A study in ideology and support base of the Congress party 1972", *Mimeographed.*
6. K.R. Acharya, *The Critical Elections: A Study of Andhra Pradesh Assembly Elections 1978*, Ramesh Publications, Hyderabad, 1979, p. 43.
7. *1980 Parliamentary Elections: State-wide Survey*, Political Science Department, Osmania University.
8. R. Yadgiri, "Congress Party and its Support Structure: A Case Study of Medak", Parliamentary Constituency 1980 (unpublished thesis).
9. Satyanarayan, "Political Communication in Andhra Pradesh: Role of Mass Media" (unpublished thesis).

10. A survey conducted by Political Science Department, Osmania University, Hyderabad, 1982-83.
11. R. Yadgiri, *op. cit.*
12. *Ibid.*, p. 344.
13. K.R. Acharya, *The Critical Elections, op. cit.*, p. 13.
14. N.G. Ranga and T. Prakasam left the Congress and formed Andhra Praja Party in 1951. In the same year Prakasam left the party and formed the state unit of Kisan Mazdoor Praja Party (KMPP). Ranga, later formed his own party: Krishikar Lok Party (KLP) in 1951. After the first general elections the KMPP was converted into a unit of the PSP. See A. Narsimha Reddy, Congress parties and politics in G. Ram Reddy, B.A.V. Sharma (Eds.), *State Government and Politics: Andhra Pradesh*, Sterling, New Delhi, 1979, pp. 219-220.
15. M. Satyanarayana Rao, "Cabinet Government in Andhra Pradesh, 1956-1980." An unpublished thesis, 1980, p. 278.
16. A. Narsimha Reddy, Congress Parties and Politics, G. Ram Reddy and B.A.V. Sharma (Eds.), *op. cit.*, p. 215.
17. D.L. Sheth (Ed.), *Citizens and Parties, Aspects of Competitive Politics in India*, Allied Publishers, Delhi, 1971, p. 159.
18. Rasheeduddin Khan, "Political Participation and Political Change in Andhra Pradesh: A Case Study including a survey of State politics, 1956-57", *Mimeographed*, 1972, Osmania University, Hyderabad, pp. 57-59.
19. Sanjeeva Reddy nationalized the Kurnool Bus Transport. Nationalization of buses in Telangana area was done long ago. The same was done in Andhra in gradation, starting with Kurnool and Guntur.
20. Rasheeduddin Khan, *op. cit.*, pp. 57-59.
21. *The Hindu*, 22 November 1971.
22. Separate Andhra agitation started for many reasons. The Telangana agitation of 1969-70 was still fresh in the minds of Andhras. They resented the idea of Andhras being in the capital city as second class citizens. The Reddys who had ruled politically for 16 years lost their influence. The landed Kammas and Rajus felt that the Land Ceiling Act was going to hit them hard. With these grievances the Andhras started the movement. The students began the movement on 24 October 1972. B.V. Subba Reddy was a spokesman of the Andhras' agitation. They resolved that Andhra should be separated. (N. Inniah, *Politics for Power: The Role of Caste and Factions in Andhra Pradesh 1880-1980*, Scientific Services, Hyderabad, 1981, p. 121).
23. *The Hindu*, December 2, 1973.
24. Rajni Kothari, *Politics in India*, Orient Longman, New Delhi, 1972, p. 192.
25. In 1946, when the nation's value system was different, Gandhiji had objected to T. Prakasam, the undisputed Andhra leader, becoming

the chief minister of Madras simply because the latter, having given up a lucrative practice at the bar to join the freedom movement, retained for himself the Rs. 30,000 purse presented to him by his admirers.

26. *The Hindu*, January 4, 1983.
27. Out of the 294 seats Congress(I) contested, I could collect from the Congress(I) State party office, Hyderabad, the caste background of 274 candidates. The caste division of 274 is: Reddy 73, Kamma 57, Kshatriya 30, Velama 6, Brahmins 11, BCs 53, Vysya 4, Harijan 22, Girijan 6, Christian 2, Muslim 10. 181 belonged to upper castes, 81 were from among weaker sections and 12 from minorities.

5

EMERGENCE OF REGIONAL PARTIES IN INDIA
Case of Telugu Desam

M. SHATRUGNA

THE emergence of Telugu Desam in Andhra Pradesh and the capture of power in Karnataka by the Janata-Kranti Ranga combine raises a number of issues in the electoral politics of the Indian polity. While a number of states like Tamil Nadu, Jammu and Kashmir, West Bengal and Tripura have been ruled by non-Congress governments for more than 5 years and the north-east states have a number of recognised regional political parties, what is the significance of the present elections in Andhra Pradesh and Karnataka? Actually regional parties outnumber "national" parties--while there are 7 national parties, recognised regional parties are 29 and unrecognised 12.

Andhra Pradesh and Karnataka have been the bastions of the Congress party since independence, playing a major role in the Congress politics at the centre. Andhra Pradesh is the largest state which has had uninterrupted Congress rule since independence. With this unique political background, what has the Congress come to in this state?

THE CRISIS IN THE CONGRESS

The crisis in the Congress appears to have been precipitated with the declaration of Emergency in June 1975 when democratic rights were not in operation. The desertion of the party by a number of leaders on the eve of the 1977 parliamentary poll left Indira Gandhi more powerful within the Congress party. The ignominous break-up of the Janata and the victory of the Congress(I) at the 1980 mid-term poll gave credibility to the Congress(I)'s assertion that there was no alternative to Indira Gandhi's party. While the people were fed up with the much publicised but little operationalised 20-point programme of Indira Gandhi and the 5-point programme of Sanjay Gandhi, there was no alternative political force to provide leadership for the general frustration and disillusionment of the people. After Sanjay's death the attempts of Indira Gandhi to bring her elder son to the cockpit of national politics only served to accentuate the functioning of what is known as *durbari* politics. The entire political machinery appeared as an extension of the family and it was generally felt that, to Indira Gandhi, the interests of her family, especially her son, were above the interests of her party and the state. Excessive centralisation of power and systematic destruction of already weak political institutions had reached such a degree that even the selection of a district Congress committee secretary in a remote Andhra district had to be cleared by the high command. The distinction between the personalised party politics and government, already so narrow, was reduced further during this period. Concentration of power in one person or family was total not only in the party but also in the functioning of the government. The prime minister's secretariat assumed added importance in this context.

Further, the distinction between the powers of the state and those of the centre as embodied in the Sixth and Seventh schedules of the Indian Constitution, tended to be obliterated with the frequent imposition of President's rule in the states. The appointment of Governors became a source of patronage and often these appointees appeared to be more the agents of the ruling party than representatives of the President of India.

THE BOGEY OF NATIONAL DISINTEGRATION

Whenever a non-Congress state was afflicted with communal

disturbances, drought or a situation of law and order, the central government intervened in the state and raised the bogey of national disintegration and external threat. In order to maintain "public order" and "national unity", it often assumed more coercive powers. The continuous presence of the Preventive Detention Act in the statute book from 1950, except briefly when Indira Gandhi had no majority in Parliament after the 1969 party split, the Maintenance of Internal Security Act (MISA), the National Security Act (NSA), the Essential Services Maintenance Act (ESMA) and their use on the opposition only served, to reinforce the view-point that the concentration of power at the centre reduces the states to a dependent status. Even with a two-thirds majority in the Lok Sabha, the Congress is unable to maintain law and order.

Andhra Pradesh has the dubious distinction of having been ruled by chief ministers appointed regularly by the high command for a long time. None of these appointed leaders had the necessary skills to run the administration and to balance factional fights within the party. Some even ran the state like their *jagirs*, receiving *nazrana*, being weighed in gold, and displaying an unashamed love of the feudal splendour and pomp in utter contempt of the people. The situation further deteriorated even after the change of the guard twice after Chenna Reddy was ousted. The poor Andhra peasant, the low-paid industrial worker, the educated middle class and the oppressed housewife wondered at this all pervading corruption and clamoured for a focus to register their protest and remove the undesirable people from the scene.

ENTRY OF TELUGU DESAM

The entry of N.T. Rama Rao into the state politics provided an alternative. NTR with 30 years of film career behind him is a household name in Andhra. Using an amazing display of grit, determination and singularity of purpose, he used cliche's like *atma gouravam* (self-respect) and *dharma yuddham* and *Kurukshetram* (epic war of Mahabharata) to convey his message to the people. He seriously believed that he was the saviour to "resurrect" the people from the Congress morass. For instance one of NTR cut-outs says *Telugu Desam pilustondi, lea. kadaliraa* [Telugu Desam is calling; arise; join (us);]

In the 1983 poll, winning a clear two-thirds majority, Telugu Desam routed not only the Congress but also the opposition parties like the Janata, BJP, Lok Dal and of course the CPI and CPI(M). The voting pattern (see Table 5.1) shows that the Telugu Desam vote was a vote against all the so-called all-India parties.

It shows that a regional party which has local roots, identifying itself with local problems can pose a successful challenge to all-India parties. The victory of Telugu Desam reveals that the regional idiom, regional language, regional problems and regional milieu are acceptable to the people notwithstanding the propaganda of the ruling all-India party that a regional party is anti-national. It also shows that leaders with grit, determination, devotion and singularity of purpose still have a place in politics. They draw a lot of admiration from the common people. The fact that NTR won both in urban and rural areas with a wide margin of votes attests this. People also seemed to like his "independence"—recall the manner in which he shunned electoral alliance with the opposition. This determination brought many to his side. NTR tried to give credibility to his actions which quality the opposition lacked. For instance the CPI, which initially wanted to have an electoral alliance with Telugu Desam but could not do so as NTR refused their demand of 60 seats, asked the people to defeat Telugu Desam in a write up in their Telugu daily *Visalandhra* on 3 January, just two days before the poll. Such opportunism cost the opposition a lot. The "national question"—language, culture, ethos, etc.—though raised by NTR in a superficial manner caught the imagination of the people. Absence of political strength among the local Congress leaders to extract their legitimate due from the centre was fully exposed by NTR in his election speeches. There was derisive laughter in the audience when he spoke about the servile nature of the successive chief ministers in the state.

TABLE 5.1: **Position of political parties in 1978 and 1983 elections**

Party	Seats contested		Seats won		Votes polled		%	
	1978	1983	1978	1983	1978	1983	1978	1983
TDP	—	288	—	198	—	97,77,066	—	46.33
Congress (I)	290	293	175	60	79,08,221	70,67,785	39.24	33.49
CPI	31	48	6	4	5,01,452	5,88,027	2.48	2.79
CPM	23	28	8	5	5,46,262	4,23,509	2.71	2.01
BJP	—	80	—	3	—	5,88,439	—	2.79
Janata	269	44	60	1	57,93,049	1,99,234	28.74	0.94
Lok Dal	—	33	—	—		1,91,862	—	0.91
Congress (J)	—	80	—	1		1,04,067	—	0.49
Congress (S)	—	9	—	—		44,522	—	0.21
Independents	NA	NA	15	21	18,72,289	21,18,070	9.29	10.04

Source: *Indian Express*, Hyderabad Edition, 24-1-1983, p. 3.

A TREND SETTER

The performance of the all-India parties like the Congress has been so dismal all these years that the electorate wanted an alternative party with new dynamic leadership. This was needed in our type of electoral politics.

The results show that decentralisation of power, local action, local expression are likely to find acceptance with the people. The emergence of Telugu Desam will give an impetus to the formation of regional parties in other states to bid for power. But such parties must first shed the trappings of secession, communalism and linguistic chauvinism. The election campaign of Telugu Desam appeared to be by and large secular. Though its detractors tried to paint it as a Kamma party, it has crossed the barriers of caste, creed and religion in its election campaign.

For instance, of the 288 contestants, upper castes have 152 candidates, weaker sections 128 and minorities 8. In turn the weaker sections have 73 in the B.C. category, Harijans 40 and Girijans 15. In other words about 53 per cent of the candidates belong to the upper castes and 45 per cent to the weaker sections. The position is different in the case of Congress(I). Whereas the upper castes have 66 per cent candidates, weaker sections constitute 33 per cent. Thus the Congress(I) list is favourable towards upper castes in comparison to the TDP list where the accommodation of weaker sections is more both in terms of percentage (45%) and absolute numbers (128) (for details see Table 5.2).

Also TDP appears to have made a serious attempt to select candidates who are educated and younger. Of the 278 candidates, whose educational background is known 28 hold post-graduate degree and 125 a degree. While 33 have Intermediate qualification, 61 have passed S.S.C. One more interesting feature is that of the qualified, 20 are medical doctors, 46 practising advocates and 7 engineers. Thus "professionals" alone constitute 27 per cent. As for age details, the statewise average age of the TDP candidates is 41. Those below 30 years are 33; between 31 and 35 years 68; 36 and 40 years 55; 41 and 50 years 80; 51 and 60 years 40; 61 and 70 years 5; and only

TABLE 5.2: **Caste-wise break-up of Telugu Desam and Congress(I) contestants in 1983 Assembly election**

Caste	Total no. of Telugu Desam candidates		Total no. of Conr. (I) candidates	
	Category-wise	Caste-wise	Category-wise	Caste-wise
1	2	3	4	5
A. *Upper castes*	152		181	
1. Reddy		65		73
2. Kamma		59		57
3. Kshatriya		13		30
4. Velama		5		6
5. Brahmins		3		11
6. Vysya		7		4
B. *Weaker sections*	128		81	
(a) Backward class				
1. Kapu		26		
2. Velama (B.C.)		10		
3. Gouda		9		
4. Yadava		6		
5. Kalinga		3		
6. Mudiraja		3		53
7. Padmasali		2		
8. Agnikula Kshatriya		2		
9. Kurma		2		
10. Balija		1		
*11. Others		9		
(b) Scheduled castes		40		22
(c) Scheduled tribes		15		6
C. *Minorities*	8			
1. Christian		2		12
2. Muslim		6		
D. *Not known*		—		19
	Total	288	Total	293

*Others : Patkara Kshatriya-2, Gavara-1, Togata-1, Jain-1, Chattada Vaishnava-1, Bhavasara Kshatriya-1, Kayasta-1, Rajput-1.

Source: Collected from Telugu Desam Party office and also from Congress (I) office in Hyderabad.

one candidate is above 70 years age. Thus while 156 candidates are below the age of 40 years (53%), those below 50 years age constitute 82 per cent of the total candidates. (for details see Table 5.3).

TABLE 5.3 : (A) Educational qualifications of Telugu Desam candidates in 1983 Assembly election

Level of Education	Frequency	% Total
Post graduates	28	10.00
Graduates	125	43.00
Intermediate	33	11.50
S.S.C.	61	21.25
Below S.S.C.	26	9.00
Hindi Pandits	2	0.70
Telugu Pandits	1	0.35
Law Diploma	1	0.35
Engg. Diploma	1	0.35
Not known	10	3.50
Total	288	100.00
(B) *Age Details*		
30 years or below	33	11.50
31 years to 35	68	23.25
36 years to 40	55	19.05
41 years to 50	80	28.00
51 years to 60	40	14.00
61 years to 70	5	1.75
Above 70 years	1	0.35
Not known	6	2.10
Total	288	100.00

Source: Telugu Desam Party office, Hyderabad.

SUMMING UP

The 26-year uninterrupted Congress rule in Andhra Pradesh came to an abrupt end with the emergence of Telugu Desam as the ruling party in the 1983 Assembly Election. Centralisation of power, weakening of political institutions, the erosion of democratic methods, the raising of the bogey of national disintegration are some of the reasons for the rejection of

Congress from the political power scene of the state. NTR's less than a year old Telugu Desam became the focus of the anti-Congressism. Decentralisation of power, local action, milieu and culture are some of the issues on which NTR won the election. The victory of Telugu Desam shows that a regional party devoid of linguistic chauvinism, casteism and separatism has a chance of coming to power, however "big and old", the so called all-India parties may be.

MANIFESTO OF TELUGU DESAM

Clean administration

"Telugu Desam", if voted to power, will remove, lock, stock and barrel, the discredited culture created by the Congress(I) and provide a clean and efficient administration. It will recognize, honour and encourage honest officials and will see that a real democratic system is fostered.

Pride of place to Telugu language

Telugu language will be given its pride of place. Telugu will be made the official language right up to the Secretariat level. It will be made the medium of instruction at the University level too. "Telugu Desam" will strive hard to restore the lost glory of Telugus and do everything for the enrichment of the Telugu language. At the same time, "Telugu Desam" will encourage and protect the language and culture of people from other states.

Aid to farmers

Agriculture is the main occupation of a vast majority of people in the state. But, presently it is in a very sorry state. Farmers are not getting remunerative prices though cost inputs have been going up. With the result, farmers are on the verge of bankruptcy. Small and marginal farmers are migrating to urban areas for sheer survival. Artisans are not able to eke out a living and are just languishing. "Telugu Desam" if voted to power, will guarantee remunerative prices for farmers, and reasonable minimum wages for agricultural labourers. Similarly, profitable avenues will be created for the upliftment of artisans. Loopholes in the Land Ceiling Act will be plugged and land reforms effectively implemented so that the landless may be benefited.

Village development

Small and cottage industries will be promoted. Projects will be taken up for all round development of the villages. Trekking long distances for a pot of potable water will be a thing of the past. Measures will be taken so that chronically drought-affected regions of the State, especially Rayalaseema are relieved of this problem. Long-term projects will be taken up for countering the vagaries of nature.

Rural electrification

Andhra Pradesh has ample scope for power generation. Despite this, ten thousand villages are still engulfed by total darkness. "Telugu Desam" will take steps for electrification of all the villages.

More powers for panchayat raj institutions

If developmental works are to be executed successfully, Panchayat Raj institutions and local bodies should work well. For this, they should be vested with sufficient power and provided with enough funds. By decentralisation of powers and authority, the "Telugu Desam" will strengthen democracy at the grass-roots level.

Basic changes in education system

The present educational system is only contributing to more unemployment. The chaos and confusion that are now prevailing in all the educational institutions right from the primary school to the University level will be removed. "Telugu Desam" will see that bright students will not put a stop to their education because of their poor economic conditions. Importance will be given to vocational and technical education so that they generate self-employment opportunities. Uniform curricula will be framed for all the Universities in the State. Strict measures will be taken to set right the conditions in Universities which are plagued by partiality, anarchy and indiscipline. Capitation system of education will be ended and only merit will be given preference. Scholarships will be liberally extended to students belonging to Scheduled Castes, Scheduled Tribes, backward classes and economically weaker sections.

Mid-day meal scheme

Mid-day meal scheme was originally conceived by "Telugu Desam" with a view to provide nutritious food to the poor children in the Primary Schools. But when the ruling party borrowed this idea to be used as an election gimmick and tried to implement it in haste, many loopholes crept in. "Telugu Desam" will evolve a scientific system to implement the Mid-day Meal Scheme quite effectively and also successfully.

Rapid industrialisation of the State

Andhra Pradesh is accorded a step-motherly treatment by the centre with regard to industrial development. In spite of having abundant natural resources, the present rulers have turned a Nelson's eye on this state. As a result of the callous attitude of the ruling party, the Vizag Steel Plant which Telugu secured by sacrificing their lives is still in an infant stage. The Mangalagiri tyre factory is yet to take shape even on paper. Though innumerable promises have been made for the industrialisation of the backward regions, nothing has been done so far. They have turned out only to be a lip service. If people vote "Telugu Desam" to power, it would take steps for the speedy execution of all these major projects. It would ensure rapid industrialisation of the state. It would fight for the due share of industries and create an environment which would attract investors living in other States as well as abroad. Red-tapism and inefficiency among the public sector undertakings would be eliminated. Taking into account the local conditions and the cost of living, "Telugu Desam" would try to raise the wages of industrial workers "Telugu Desam" would take all the measures for the welfare of the workers who occupy a significant place in the economic development of the country.

Medical and health services

"Telugu Desam" is determined to provide medical and health benefits to all sections of the people. It would raise the budget allocations for medical and health services and see that there is no shortage of man-power nor scarcity of equipment in the Primary Health Centres, Taluk and District hospitals. It will attach importance for providing modern equipment and raising the bed strength in hospitals.

To contain population explosion, "Telugu Desam" will adopt persuasive methods for accepting family planning as a way of life instead of compulsive measures.

Reforming the police force

The police force in Andhra Pradesh is very much discredited under the Congress rule. Law and order is fast deteriorating. "Telugu Desam" will cleanse the police force the moment it comes to power. Obstacles faced by honest officials in the discharge of their duties will be removed. It will see that there is no scope for political interference in the functioning of the Police. It will look after the welfare of the Police and provide modern equipment for the efficient performance of their duties. It will reorganise the entire police force in such a manner that the activities of the anti-social elements will be ruthlessly curbed and people will repose confidence in the Police Department.

Timely completion of projects

Construction and completion of irrigation projects have progressed at a snail's pace under the Congress Governments. Projects initiated 25 years back are yet to be completed. Other states were able to complete their projects by bringing pressure on the centre and by getting aid from World Bank and other agencies. But the Congress(I) Government exhibited a callous negligence in this regard which is unpardonable. Though people in Rayalaseema have been making a demand for decades for the diversion of the Krishna waters for their parched lands, nothing has been done so far for their benefit. If "Telugu Desam" wins the elections, it would hasten the process of construction of Srisailam canals.

Women's welfare

"Telugu Desam" will see that women's welfare does not remain a mere slogan. It will guarantee their legitimate rights. It condemns the feudal culture which only views women as objects of pleasure. It would initiate action for equal share for daughters in the paternal property along with the sons. It would establish a separate University for women and would ensure a respectable place for women in the society. The evil practice of dowry will be curbed.

Encouragement to youth

"Telugu Desam" will give special importance to youth—the hope of future India. It will prepare projects which will channellise abundant energies of the youth for constructive activities. It will do its best to relieve the youth from the tentacles of unemployment. As a beginning, it would take up projects which would ensure one job per family. It will introduce self-employment schemes in villages to the enthusiastic youth and artisans.

The party will promote sports and promising sportsmen will be given scholarship. Provision for employment of sportsmen and women in educational institutions will be made. Every district will have a stadium. Promotion of games and sports in villages will be given priority.

Centre-State relations

"Telugu Desam" will work according to the spirit of the federal character of the Constitution which ensures greater autonomy to the States. "Telugu Desam" will oppose Delhi rulers imposing their decisions on Andhra Pradesh. Only defence, foreign affairs, currency and communications should be under the purview of the Central Government. "Telugu Desam" believes that Centre-State relations are interdependent and a strong Centre emerges only when States enjoy more powers. "Telugu Desam", after coming to power, would establish a High Power Committee to go into the question of Centre-State relations including clear demarcation of powers and to suggest necessary constitutional amendments, if necessary.

Dedication to democracy

"Telugu Desam" will fight for the protection of democracy. It will uphold moral values, democratic traditions, and see that all the citizens enjoy individual freedom benefiting a civilized society. "Telugu Desam" will not do anything to deprive the citizens of the fundamental rights guaranteed by the Constitution. It will fight for the withdrawal of black legislations such as NSA and ESMA. "Telugu Desam" feels that no person should hold two posts except under unavoidable circumstances.

Autonomy for radio and TV

It is the firm belief of the party that Doordarshan and All-India Radio should be autonomous. Till such time "Telugu Desam" demands that these two instruments of mass communication should be handed over to their respective states. "Telugu Desam" will strive for the establishment of more centres of AIR and Doordarshan. "Telugu Desam" strongly opposes the present tendency of this media in distorting the facts contrary to public opinion and to suit the interests of the ruling party at the centre.

Freedom of the press

"Telugu Desam" is totally committed to the Freedom of the Press, and it gives a solemn assurance to the Fourth Estate that it will not come in the way of free and fearless functioning of the press under any circumstances. Further, the Party will strive to bring an amendment to the Constitution to make Press Freedom as a fundamental right.

Independence of judiciary

"Telugu Desam" will do its best for the elevation of judiciary to a higher plane. It will not interfere in appointment, promotion and transfer of judges. It will strive for cordial relations between the executive and the judiciary.

Electoral reforms

"Telugu Desam," within its own purview will strive for comprehensive electoral reforms. The "Telugu Desam" feels that the present trend, where money-power alone wins the elections should go. The government should bear the expenses of electioneering of the candidates so that honest candidates can contest and win. It also demands the audit of the election expenses of all the parties by the Election Commission. The People's Representation Act should be so amended that the party in power will not commit fraud against the people and the electorate. Elections should not be postponed for more than three months and elections should not also be preponed.

Anti defection

Political defections have reached ominous proportions. "Telugu Desam" firmly opposes the defection game, which is why it has insisted on MLAs wishing to join "Telugu Desam" that they have to resign their elective posts first and only then join the party. This healthy precedent should be followed by an enactment whereby membership of the legislative bodies automatically gets cancelled, the moment the concerned person defects. With a view to set an example that "Telugu Desam" practises what it preaches, the party is asking its candidates to take an oath in public that they would resign their elective posts in the event of their joining other parties in future.

Curb on government expenditure

"Telugu Desam" will take effective steps to reduce government expenditure at executive level. It will also see that public money is not squandered on ministerial visits and official extravaganza. Many government corporations and boards which do not serve any purpose and which have become white elephants will be abolished.

A kilogram of rice for rupees 2

"Telugu Desam" will strengthen the public distribution system and will see that the essential commodities are made available to the people at very reasonable rates. It is the firm resolve of "Telugu Desam" to ensure sale of a kilogram of rice for rupees two.

Rational tax structure

The present tax system is nothing but robbing Paul to pay Peter. "Telugu Desam" will restructure the whole tax system on a rational basis. Honest traders will be protected from the menace of corrupt officials. At the same time hoarders, black-marketeers and corrupt officials will be severely punished.

Priority to housing

"Telugu Desam" will take up a massive house construction programme all over the State, both in the cities and in the villages. Special housing schemes will be taken up for weaker sections and industrial and agricultural labourers. Similarly, "Telugu Desam" will take up a project by which every government employee will own a house by the time he reaches the age of fifty.

Secularism

"Telugu Desam" will observe secularism enshrined in our Constitution in letter and spirit. It will take special care with regard to minorities and see that all the privileges guaranteed by the Constitution are provided to them. It will discuss with educationists and take measures for the promotion of Urdu language. "Telugu Desam" will ensure that all those who live in the state enjoy equal rights, privileges and opportunities irrespective of their caste, religion or state of origin.

Development of backward classes

It is the firm belief of the party that people belonging to backward classes, who have been oppressed for centuries should draw special attention from the government. "Telugu Desam" will see that the privileges guaranteed by the Constitution with regard to education, employment, etc., are extended to them in practice. "Telugu Desam" will protect the Harijans, the Tribals and other down-trodden sections of the society from the atrocities of the dominant castes and official excesses. Excise system will be amended to benefit the toddy-tappers. It will also take measures for the development of fisheries and initiate a comprehensive package deal for the upliftment of fishermen. Finance will be made available to rickshaw pullers for the purchase of rickshaws.

Aid to handloom industry

"Telugu Desam" will take all measures to strengthen and develop the cooperative movement in handloom sector which is playing a vital role in rural economy by providing the cotton yarn and establishing the necessary infrastructure to market their products.

Elections to the municipal corporation of Hyderabad

In the past Hyderabad was famous for its beauty and cleanliness. But under the Congress rule the city not only lost its beauty and cleanliness but also became notorious as a city of inconveniences. The ruling party has been postponing elections for the Municipal Corporation of Hyderabad for quite some time. "Telugu Desam" is determined to conduct elections to this body soon after coming to power. The party will do its best to improve civic amenities for the citizens.

"Telugu Desam" looks forward to making Andhra Pradesh highly prosperous with enormous agricultural wealth, industrial advancement, rapid strides in the field of education and cultural resurgence. It is determined to uphold the honour and prestige of the Telugu people and to revive the glory of their proud heritage.

Corruption under the Congress rule has reached alarming proportions. Inefficiency is at its peak. Maladministration is ubiquitous. The net result is that Andhra Pradesh is allowed to degenerate by the self-centred Congress rulers inspite of the fact that nature has been so kind in bestowing the state with a lot of resources. "Telugu Desam" takes a solemn pledge that it would lead Andhra Pradesh towards allround prosperity making optimum utilisation of its abundant natural resources. "Telugu Desam" is quite confident that the people of Andhra Pradesh would drive out the corrupt Congress(I) from the state by casting their invaluable votes in favour of "Telugu Desam" with which they have identified themselves, extending overwhelming affection and patronage.

Jai Telugu Nadu !
Jai Hind ! !

6

SOCIAL BACKGROUND OF TELUGU DESAM LEGISLATORS

G. SRINIVAS, M. SHATRUGNA &
G. NARAYANA

THE Telugu Desam Party won the 1983 Assembly elections with two-thirds majority to the surprise of many of its supporters and opponents. It is significant to note here that the party within a short period of six months of its origin could develop tactics to beat the impregnable fortress of Congress(I). While earlier analysis pointed out the uniqueness of the election campaign of TDP and also the particular circumstances which led to the decline and fall of the ruling Congress party, there were a few other significant factors to be taken into account. One among these is the selection of candidates for the constituencies. All political parties, irrespective of their ideological differences, take into account complex factors like caste, age, educational qualifications, money power and previous political experience into consideration before accepting the nomination of a particular candidate to contest the election on party ticket. It is this combination of factors in the selection process in addition to other political realities, that makes the party win or lose the elections. The selection of candidates by the Telugu Desam Party could strike a better balance among different interest groups than the other well-established parties.

This paper attempts briefly to look into the caste affiliation, age and educational qualifications (district-wise) of TDP legislators and a comparative analysis of their social background and organisational experiences with the Congress party in Andhra Pradesh in the previous legislature.

A lot of publicity was given by the TDP and the mass media, notably, *Eenadu*, a Telugu daily, that only candidates with a clean record and good academic qualifications would be given party tickets in the elections. The TDP compiled the bio-data of all its candidates. The following analysis indicates that TDP in comparison with the Congress(I) had fielded more candidates from the middle castes and backward classes; it had younger and educationally more highly qualified candidates.

Caste affiliation of candidates

Caste as a status group determining the hierarchical interactions and interrelationships in traditional India has, in the post-independence era, been transformed into a political group to articulate the social and economic interests. So, increasingly the caste affiliation of the position seekers became important at the time of elections. The caste group numerically dominant in a particular constituency, or a combination of caste groups have considerable influence on the election outcome. In Andhra politics, caste always played a predominant role in regional politics. So it was not surprising that the leaders of Congress(I) tried to discredit the Telugu Desam Party by branding it as the party of Kammas—one of the dominant groups in Andhra. However, this was not reflected in a major way with regard to the selection of party candidates. On the other hand the TDP, unlike others, depended more on the backward classes or a combination of backward classes and dominant caste groups in the region.

Of the 203 candidates who won on the Telugu Desam Party ticket, the caste affiliation of 194 was available. (See Table 6.1).

These caste groups are divided into five major categories: One, representing the upper castes like Brahmins and Vaisyas; and second, the middle castes like Velama, Reddy, Raju and Kamma; the third, the backward classes like Kapu, Telaga,

TABLE 6.1 : **Caste affiliation of the Telugu Desam Party legislators, 1983**

S. No.	Caste status	No. of legislators	Total
A.	*Upper Castes*		6
	1. Brahmins	3	
	2. Vaisya	3	
B.	*Middle Castes*		101
	1. Kamma	43	
	2. Reddy	43	
	3. Raju	12	
	4. Velama	3	
C.	*Backward Classes*		54
	1. Kapu	13	
	2. Telaga	6	
	3. Golla	7	
	4. Gouda	4	
	5. Balija	3	
	6. Other Backward Classes	21	
D.	*Scheduled castes*	25	25
E.	*Scheduled tribes*	5	5
F.	*Minority communities*	3	3
	Total	194	194

Golla, Gouda, Balija and others; fourth, the Scheduled Castes; and fifth the Scheduled Tribes. Of the 194 legislators, nearly one-third are drawn from the backward classes. While the backward classes category represents various small sub-castes, single dominant group among them is that of Kapus with 13 representatives in the legislature. Immediately followed by the backward classes are the dominant middle caste groups. Among them more importance was given to Kammas and Reddis. All these groups put together won more than half of the total Telugu Desam seats in the Assembly. There is hardly any representation here of the upper castes.

The selection of the candidates also reflects the numerical strength of these caste groups in each district. While some of the caste groups like Reddi, Kamma and Kapu are widespread, a few others like Raju, Velama, Telaga and Golla are confined to a few districts. So it is clear that each district has been taken as a unit for the selection of candidates (see Table 6.2).

TABLE 6.2 : **Caste Status and regionwise representation of Telugu Desam Party Legislators**

Name of caste	Coastal districts no. of MLAs	Rayalaseema no. of MLAs	Telangana no. of MLAs	Total no. of MLAs
Brahmin	1	—	2	3
Vaisya	2	1	—	3
Kamma	29	8	6	43
Reddy	14	19	10	43
Raju	11	1	—	12
Velama	—	—	3	3
Kapu	9	2	2	13
Telaga	6	—	—	6
Golla	6	—	1	7
Gouda	2	1	1	4
Balija	1	1	1	3
Other BCs	16	2	3	21
Scheduled Castes	14	7	4	25
Scheduled Tribes	4	—	1	5
Minorities	—	2	1	3
Total	115	44	35	194

From the analysis of Table 6.2, it is also clear that the Telugu Desam Party had a strategy to bring an alliance between dominant caste groups and backward classes together and depended heavily on the numerical strength of these groups in a particular constituency for support and votes. This is in contrast to the then ruling party's combination of the upper caste groups and the Scheduled Castes and Tribes.

Age of the legislators

Age of the legislators is another indicator of the strategy followed at the time of elections. In the pre-poll advertisements for candidates, the Telugu Desam Party had explicitly stated that emphasis would be on the young aspirants. This was translated into practice (see Table 6.3) Many of the legislators elected on the Telugu Desam Party tickets were very young.

TABLE 6.3 : **Districtwise age of Telugu Desam Party Legislators**

Name of the district	Age : Number of years						
	26-30	31-35	36-40	41-45	46-50	51-55	Total
Srikakulam	5	1	1	1	3	—	11
Vijayanagaram	2	2	—	1	1	2	8
Vizag	2	3	1	2	—	3	11
E. Godavari	1	4	6	4	3	1	19
W. Godavari	2	—	2	3	1	5	13
Krishna	2	1	4	—	1	2	10
Guntur	1	1	5	—	4	4	15
Prakasam	1	1	3	1	2	1	9
Nellore	—	1	1	1	—	2	5
Chittoor	1	2	1	1	1	4	10
Cudappa	—	2	—	—	—	—	2
Anantapur	—	3	2	3	3	1	12
Kurnool	—	2	2	—	4	—	8
Mahboobnagar	—	1	1	—	—	2	4
Ranga Reddy	—	—	—	—	—	—	—
Hyderabad	1	—	3	2	—	—	6
Medak	—	—	—	1	—	—	1
Nizamabad	—	5	—	—	1	—	6
Adilabad	—	1	—	—	1	1	3
Karimnagar	—	1	2	—	1	—	4
Warangal	—	—	—	1	1	—	2
Khammam	—	—	—	—	1	—	1
Nalgonda	2	1	—	1	—	—	4
Total	20	32	34	22	28	28	164

The age of 164 legislators was analysed. The legislators are divided into seven categories with a 5-year interval between each category. Nearly half of them belong to below 40 years age group, while the other half belong to the middle age group. There are only seven members who are above 60 years, of which the founder President of Telugu Desam Party is one. The average age of the legislators is slightly below 40 years. This also indicates that many are entering the legislature without any previous political experience of local bodies. We discuss this in detail towards the later part of this paper (see Tables 6.9 and 6.11).

The age of 157 TDP MLAs was compared to the Congress(I) MLAs of 1978. This comparative study showed that there were more young people, that is, those who were below 40 years in the present ruling party than there were in 1978. TDP had 38 per cent of its legislators who were below 40 years, while

TABLE 6.4 : Age of the legislators in the ruling parties in 1978 and 1983

Age	Legislators	
	Congress 1978 N=251	Telugu Desam 1983 N=197
25-29	11 (4.3)	18 (9.1)
30-34	31 (12.3)	23 (11.6)
35-39	22 (8.7)	34 (17.2)
40-44	34 (13.9)	20 (10.1)
45-49	35 (13.9)	33 (16.8)
50-54	40 (15.9)	11 (5.5)
55-59	17 (6.7)	10 (5)
60-64	16 (6.3)	6 (3)
65-69	2 (0.7)	1 (0.5)
70-74	1 (0.3)	1 (0.5)
N.A.	42 (16.7)	40 (20.3)
Total	251 (100)	197 (100)

Note : Figures in brackets are percentages.

Source : The data on the Congress(I) and Telugu Desam legislators in this Table and the following Tables were computed from "Who's Who" by Andhra Pradesh legislature Secretariat and TDP profiles of the party headquarters respectively.

the Congress(I) had only 25 per cent of its legislators in this age group. 30 per cent of the legislators in the Congress(I) were in the age group of above 50 years, while the TDP had only 14 per cent of its MLAs in this age group (see Table 6.4). The results show that TDP had succeeded in projecting itself as a party of young political aspirants. This had many implications for the election campaign and also for the image of the party in the electorate: one, the selection of young members meant the introduction of dynamism into politics and also freeing it from corruption, and second, it also meant that the dynamism of young aspirants would be harnessed for the development of the state. So, many of these positive projections had considerable effect on the electorate.

Educational background of legislators

There was a general impression among people that the elected members were either less educated or illiterate. This was particularly so when people talk about the performance of legislators in the assembly. However, this general perception had been proved wrong in the case of Telugu Desam legislators. They were not only highly educated but also largely drawn from a professional background. This was particularly significant keeping in view that the literacy rate in Andhra Pradesh was only 29.94 when compared to the national average of 36.17 according to the 1981 Census. Of the 197 legislators, information in regard to the educational qualifications of 164 was available. They have been divided into four major categories: one, below matric; second, equivalent to Matriculation; third, with graduate and post-graduate qualifications; and fourth, professional degree holders (see Table 6.5).

How did the electorate respond to the educationally qualified candidates of TDP? Of the 293 candidates that the TDP fielded, the educational background of 278 have been analysed. We find that a high percentage of graduates (61%) and professional (66%) who were given tickets got elected. This was also the case with candidates who had Intermediate qualifications (see Table 6.6). However, only 30 per cent of the candidates who had been educated up to the school level were elected.

TABLE 6.5 : **Districtwise educational qualifications of Telugu Desam Party MLAs**

Name of the district	Educational qualifications				
	Below matric	Matric/ S.S.L.C.	Graduation/ P. gradua-tion	Profes-sional degree	Total
Srikakulam	1	2	3	5	11
Vijayanagaram	3	3	2	—	8
Vizag	1	4	5	2	12
E. Godavari	3	5	8	3	19
W. Godavari	2	3	4	3	12
Krishna	—	3	5	2	10
Guntur	—	5	2	7	14
Prakasam	4	4	—	1	9
Nellore	2	2	—	1	5
Chittoor	1	3	3	3	10
Cudappa	—	—	2	2	4
Anantapur	—	4	3	4	11
Kurnool	3	3	—	2	8
Mahboobnagar	1	—	—	3	4
Ranga Reddy	—	—	—	—	—
Hyderabad	—	1	—	4	5
Medak	—	—	1	—	1
Nizamabad	—	3	1	2	6
Adilabad	—	2	—	1	3
Karimnagar	—	3	—	1	4
Warangal	—	1	—	2	3
Khammam	—	1	—	—	1
Nalgonda	—	1	2	1	4
Total	21	53	41	49	164

Further, the educational qualifications of the legislators in the ruling party now are of a higher standard than those of the ruling party legislators in 1978.

Fortynine per cent of the Telugu Desam Legislators, that is, nearly half of them are either professionals or graduates and postgraduates, while legislators with such academic qualifications accounted for only 43 per cent in the 1978 Congress legislature party (see Table 6.7). The percentage of those who had schooling and Intermediate qualification are more in the

TABLE 6.6 : **Education level of Telugu Desam Party candidates—Losers and winners**

Education	TDP candidates		
	Candidates given tickets	Candidates who won	Candidates who lost
Schooling	91 (100)	27 (29.7)	64 (70.3)
Inter and vocational	34 (100)	26 (76.5)	8 (23.5)
Graduates and post-graduates	80 (100)	49 (61.3)	31 (38.6)
Professional educated	73 (100)	48 (65.8)	25 (34.2)

Note : Figures in brackets are percentages.

TABLE 6.7 : **Education of legislators of the ruling parties—1978 and 1983**

Education	Party	
	Congress 1978 N=251	Telugu Desam 1983 N=197
Schooling	39 (15.5)	27 (13.7)
Intermediate and Vocational	14 (5.6)	26 (13.2)
Graduates and Post-graduates	48 (19.1)	49 (24.9)
Professionals	59 (23.5)	48 (24.4)
N.A.	91 (36.3)	49 (23.6)
Total	251 (100)	197 (100)

Note: Figures in brackets are percentages.

Telugu Desam Party (27%) than in the party which had come into power in 1978 (21%).

The major group of legislators are from among the science and arts graduates and post-graduates. These two groups together account for more than half of the elected legislators. On the other hand, there are only 14 persons whose education level is less than matric. This undoubtedly leads us to the conclusion that the selection of TDP candidates was more in favour of the educated political aspirants.

A majority of the legislators in the ruling party then and now are agriculturists. While there was a higher percentage of lawyers in the Congress legislature party (14%) when compared to the present ruling party (12.7%) there are more doctors in the present ruling party (6%) than they were in the Congress party (4%) in 1978. Significantly, for the first time traders have a larger representation in the ruling party. They account for 9 per cent of the Telugu Desam Party legislators. In the previous ruling party traders accounted for only 4.4 per cent (See Table 6.8).

TABLE 6.8 : **Occupation of the legislators of the ruling parties—1978 and 1983**

Occupation	Party	
	Congress 1978 N=251	Telugu Desam 1983 N=197
Agriculturists	139 (55.4)	85 (43.1)
Lawyers	35 (14)	25 (12.7)
Traders	11 (4.4)	18 (9 1)
Doctors	10 (4)	12 (6.1)
Teachers	1 (.4)	6 (3)
Government servants	—	4 (2)
Others	(.4) (1.6)	8 (4.1)
N.A.	51 (20.1)	39 (19.8)
Total	251 (100)	197 (100)

Note: Figures in brackets are percentages.

The fact that there is a higher representation of professionals, especially medical doctors, is significant because professionals usually prefer to remain apolitical. This new trend reflects, among other things, the growing interest of professionals in local and regional politics. Traditionally the representation in legislatures has been from among the legal practitioners but now their dominant position has been threatened by the entry of other professional groups into politics.

The Telugu Desam is not only a very new party but very few of its members are defectors from other parties. This is reflected in the fact that 39 per cent of its legislators have had no previous political background at all. However, 43 per cent of the Telugu Desam Party legislators have had village, municipal and district level political experience, whereas for the Congress party in the previous government this figure was 41 per cent (See Table 6.9).

TABLE 6.9 : **Previous political experience of the legislators in the ruling parties—1978 and 1983**

Previous political experience	Party	
	Congress 1978 N=251	Telugu Desam 1983 N=197
None	66 (26.3)	76 (38.6)
National level	8 (3.2)	4 (2)
State level	73 (29.1)	32 (16.2)
Village, district and municipal level	104 (41.4)	85 (43.1)
Total	251 (100)	197 (100)

Note: Figures in brackets are percentages.

This in itself is a very interesting phenomenon, in the sense that local candidates belonging to the villages and towns, with some political experience albeit, often of a non-party type have been given the party ticket, fulfilling the aspirations of the people living in those areas. This is in sharp contrast to the centralised decision making of the Congress party, which in many cases imposed outsiders on the various constituencies.

The Congress party has many legislators who have had legislative tenure both at the national and state level in comparison to the Telugu Desam Party (See Table 6.9). Predicably, the Congress with its long history has more legislators who have had previous political experience at the state and national levels in its ranks than in the fledgling nine-months old Telugu Desam Party.

Table 6.9 also shows that relatively, there are more legislators who have no previous political experience in the Telugu Desam fold than in the Congress party. This strategy by itself may have worked in the elections for the simple reason that people were fed up with the known leaders who have not done much for them in terms of removing their socio-economic backwardness and wanted to give a chance to new political aspirants under the charismatic leadership of N.T. Rama Rao.

In comparison with Telugu Desam legislators (24%) more Congress party legislators (34%) had connections with the co-operative movement in 1978 (See Table 6.10)

TABLE 6.10 : **Association of legislators of the ruling parties with the co-operative movement—1978 and 1983**

Co-operative affiliation	Party	
	Congress N=251	Telugu Desam N=197
Yes	86	47
	(34.3)	(23.9)
None	165	150
	(65.7)	(76.1)
Total	251	197
	(100)	(100)

Note: Figures in brackets are percentages.

This is to be expected of the Congress party legislators, as co-operatives in the rural sector play a powerful role both in giving credit and in production and marketing functions. Of course, political leverage is an important consideration in the dispensation of patronage involved in the sanction of loans. The resources of the co-operatives, therefore, act as a tool in the hands of the politicians. Hence it is but natural that more Congress party legislators should have associated themselves with the cooperative movement, than the ruling party legislators now, a significant number of whom are newcomers to politics itself (See Table 6.10).

TABLE 6.11 : **Association of legislators with trade union cultural and welfare organisations, student unions and professional associations—1978 and 1983**

Organisational background	Party	
	Congress N=251	Telugu Desam N=197
None	91 (36.2)	123 (62.4)
With trade unions	18 (7.2)	13 (6.6)
Student associations	11 (4.4)	14 (7.1)
Social, cultural and welfare associations	122 (48.6)	42 (21.3)
Professional associations	9 (3.6)	5 (2.5)
Total	251 (100)	197 (100)

Note: Figures in brackets are percentages.

We looked into the cultural and welfare organisations with which the legislators were associated (See Table 6.11) and found that a lower percentage of Telugu Desam legislators (21%) were associated with them in comparison to the 1978 Congress legislature party (48%). 62 per cent of the Telugu Desam legislators have no association with organisations of any kind whereas this figure was 36 per cent for the Congress party in 1978.

It is clear from the information given above, that the Congress legislators have more affiliation to the voluntary organisations and associations of different varieties compared to the Telugu Desam legislators. This may be due to two possible reasons: (1) the Congress party gives importance to those position seekers who have established their relationship with the cooperative bodies and other associations; or (2) the party culture is such that the party legislators are forced to acquire these affiliations to further consolidate their position within the party.

However, Telugu Desam legislators have had more association (7%) with student organisations than the Congress party legislators (4%). Legislators from the ruling party in both 1978 and 1983 seem equally involved in both trade unions and professional associations (see Table 6.11).

CONCLUSION

One of the most important achievements of the TDP has been that it could strike a balance between various caste groups with emphasis on backward classes in the state. This is a refreshing departure from the position of the Congress(I) which relied heavily on upper/middle castes and SCs and STs.

A relatively younger age-group of legislators has taken the reigns of the Andhra Pradesh Legislative Assembly. Nearly 50 per cent of the legislators are graduates and professionals in comparison with the 42 per cent of the Congress legislature party in 1978 which depended more on experienced than on educated politicians.

A majority of the legislators in the ruling party then and now are agriculturists. Lawyers were more in number in the Congress party, when compared to the present day ruling party. Significantly, however, Telugu Desam seems to have introduced more traders (although their numbers are small compared to other groups) into the present Assembly. The traders have increased their percentage from around 4 per cent in 1978, in the then ruling party, to a little over 9 per cent in the present ruling party.

The Telugu Desam Party legislators lack previous political experience and have limited connections with the co-operative movement, and cultural and welfare organisations. This is because of their relatively new entry into politics and public life, compared to the veteran Congressmen.

This lack of political experience among members of the Telugu Desam Party was of course an asset in the elections since, unlike the Congress legislators, they had not as yet acquired "reputations" (very often negative), which came from association with co-operatives and organisational work of various kinds in public life.

Thus, the people voted for a younger set of better educated candidates with clean records. At the moment "clean records" seem mostly a matter of political inexperience.

7

SYMBOLIC IMAGERY USED BY THE TELUGU DESAM IN ANDHRA ELECTIONS (1983)*

RATNA NAIDU

THE name "Telugu Desam Party", on the face of it appears to be regional or separatist. However, when one looks closely into the multitude of symbolic imageries with which Nandamuri Taraka Rama Rao (founder of the Telugu Desam Party henceforth referred to as "NTR") bombarded the electorate in the January 1983 elections in Andhra Pradesh, one is astonished to find the extent to which these imageries recall the composite culture which is the heritage of India. There is nothing regional in the symbolic imagery employed by the new-found Telugu Desam Party in the recent Andhra Pradesh Assembly elections. The symbols representing the just ruler and the good government taken from the roles played by NTR in movies and projected by implication as promises to the electorate of Andhra Pradesh are emotionally and culturally very much an integral part of the idiom and imagery common to the Hindi belt. The Telugu Desam movement is, in other words, very different from the DMK in Tamil Nadu which was and still is culturally a more fundamental kind of break-away movement and has been, at least, in phases, irredentist in its inclinations.

*I thank Sarat, Usha and Sarita for their help in translating from Telugu and G. Srinivas and Parda Saradhy for their kind help in collecting the election campaign material.

Growing economic disparities, extensive political fragmentation, the remarkable cultural revival brought about by the media revolution and self government during the last 35 years and the consequent sanscritization, de-sanscritization (as in the Dravidar Iyakkam) processes, or other kinds of psychocultural emphasis (as in Assam or in the Akali demands) depending on the culture area, are some of the background features of India in the 1980s which one has to keep in mind in analysing the NTR phenomenon. I speak of the "NTR phenomenon" because it is his personality which acted as the catalyst to activate processes of change which seem (in hindsight) immanent now not merely in the political situation of Andhra Pradesh but in the logic of the centre-state relations in the sub-continent as a whole. There are authorities on this subject[1] and I need not go into this here, but suffice it to mention that the slow erosion of the federal principle by one-party rule and other related factors, especially since 1971, required corrective mechanisms. Vital policy decisions determining the fate of millions on the sub-continent have ceased to be a result of the political process of bargaining and compromise. The will of a far-away centre is often sought to be implemented through puppet regimes at times against the basic interests of the people of the states. It is inevitable that the dynamics of a democratic system should reorient such a state of affairs.

However the NTR personality is important for understanding the specifics of the situation. It may be recalled that NTR was at the height of his film career and fame when he formed the Telugu Desam Party. He had acted in more than 300 films and had always preferred to play mythological roles portraying gods and goodness. His is a household name in every nook and corner of Andhra Pradesh. He is reputedly a wealthy man, well-known for his strict discipline and capacity for hard work in the 35 years of his film career. Why would such a man renounce all this and enter politics? Many times during the campaign he himself answered this question thus:

> I did not come here for money. I did not come here for status and prestige. I enjoyed all this and more. I came here as a *sanyasi* to follow you. I have earned money. I have status. And all because you gave it to me.[2]

He repeatedly reiterates that he owes his wealth, fame and triumphs to the people and gives the impression of being obsessed with the idea that he must reciprocate and serve the Telugu people in their hour of darkness. This need of the hour is articulated in the introduction to the Telugu Desam Party Manifesto as follows:

> The 35-year Congress misrule has created such a mess that the Telugus have to hang their heads in shame. Despite overwhelming majority of the ruling party in the State Assembly, political instability has become the order of the day. The enthronement of four and dethronement of three Chief Ministers within a span of five years is an indication of the sorry state of affairs. The elected representatives of the people have become mere pawns. They have neither the power to elect their leader nor to impeach him. Nor is all well with the opposition which are hopelessly divided leaving the field free for the Congress(I) to rule the roost. There is no limit to the injustice meted out to the people of the State. It is because of this historical necessity 'Telugu Desam' has come into existence in Andhra Pradesh.

For researchers interested in the ethnic dimension, the January 1983 election in Andhra Pradesh will remain a memorable one. The Congress party had been in power in Andhra Pradesh for the last 35 years, in fact since the first time elections were held in the state. More importantly, the people of the state, the Telugus, have been the most loyal supporters of Indira Gandhi throughout the turmoil—before, during, and after the Emergency years. Indeed, it may not be out of place to recall that Indira Gandhi, a lady from the northern-most state of Kashmir, represents a constituency in Andhra Pradesh in the *Lok Sabha*, and in the last national election her party won 41 of the 42 seats from Andhra Pradesh. The Telugu Desam Party formed only nine months earlier swept out Indira Gandhi's party by winning 202 seats out of a total of 294 seats in the state legislature. Significantly 35 per cent of the Telugu Desam candidates who won in the election are new entrants into politics. Telugu Desam candidates in the election had an average age of 41 years as against the Congress(I)'s 50 years.

One hundred and twenty-five of the TDP candidates were graduates, 28 post-graduates, 20 doctors, 8 engineers, and 47 lawyers. These relatively young, well educated, more or less new entrants into politics routed the Congress party candidates with such lethal slogans as *jaati gouravam* (honour of the Telugu race), *atma gouravam* (self-respect), *Teluguvalla goppatanam* (the great heritage of the Telugu people). While the imagery used by NTR in the election campaign was drawn from the all-India composite culture, clearly the appeal of the Telugu Desam (translated, Telugu Country) Party is based on regional aspirations, especially with reference to the various aspects of centre-state relations, namely finance and hierarchy in power relations.

The election campaign was a colourful and fun-filled affair. The grim questions about the non-performance of successive Congress governments were articulated through innuendos, projective implications and by analogous reference to India's rich pantheon of heroes since mythological times—kings, politicians, saints who sacrificed their all for the common man and in turn were cherished by him as models for all time to come. Slogans like *garibi hatao*, secularism or national integration, and so on were not couched in abstract terms smacking of western ideological inheritances, but it was emphasised that these radical ideas were central to the cultural inheritance of India. And NTR reminded the electorate that he had played these roles for their entertainment during the last so many decades, and that if elected he would like to activate these noble ideas, emotions and perspectives in the governance of the state.

Pamphlets, cassettes, posters, produced with all the professional expertise which might be expected of a movement led by a man who has dominated the media for many years captured the emotional and aesthetic antennae of the electorate. There were cassettes which mimicked the *faux pas* of the Anjaiahs of previous governments in songs, parody and poetry. There were other cassettes which recalled the songs of the patriot Gurajada Appa Rao and plays and other works of Kandukuri Veerasalingam. These social reformers had urged the Telugu people to give equal rights to women, to discontinue dowry and so on. We may note that the counterparts of Gurajada and Kandukuri had emerged in other regions of India at that time (as, for instance, Raja Ram Mohan Roy and others in the Brahmo Samaj movement in West Bengal). The cassettes also referred to the story of Alluri Sitarama Raju (the Bhagat Singh of Andhra) in *burrakatha*. Interspersed with such songs and *burrakatha*, the cassettes recorded NTR's speeches in which he lamented that in the land where Gurajada had left his footprints, the land which is soaked in the blood of Alluri, the land which has produced Nannayya, Tikkanna and Errapragada—the trinity that translated Vyasa's Mahabharata into Telugu, and more recently Potti Sri Ramulu and Prakasam, a land which had produced such poets, social reformers and heroes, now has leaders who are selling its pride and prestige and self-respect on the streets of Delhi.

Clearly NTR appealed in these speeches to the primordial instincts of the electorate. One is reminded that the Telugu Renaissance Movement was first exploited by the Left parties in Andhra Pradesh. But the professional skill of an NTR and his colleagues from the world of movies lent a finesse to the appeal to these primordial instincts which is unsurpassed in the history of election campaigns in the state.

The pamphlets and life-size posters projected imagery which by implication promised good and clean government. I examined one booklet which was priced and widely distributed. It is produced in colour and shows NTR with folded hands on the backcover with the inscription "Vijayasarathi"—victorious leader of Telugu Desam. The booklet consists of seven pictures of mythological and historical roles which NTR has played. In between the portraits are brief write-ups characterizing these roles. The pictures are those of NTR in the role of Krishna, Karna, Bhishma, Veera Brahmendra Swamy, Sri Krishna Devaraya, Sri Rama, and Brahma Nayadu—in that order. It can be seen that all-India mythological figures, together with more recent and local saints and beloved kings and rulers are depicted in these pictures. The brief write-ups on these figures convey selective messages about them. Lord Krishna (incarnation of Vishnu) worshipped in several worlds, appeared on this earth as protector of the innocent and destroyer of the wicked when "the earth was burdened with sin and the elements were losing their rhythm." He is the same

Krishna who is shrewd in the political arena, who guided the Pandavas, and helped justice and destroyed evil. Krishna's role *vis-a-vis* the plight of Draupadi and his role in giving shelter to 16,000 young women who were being persecuted by the Rakshasas are emphasised.

Sri Rama showed that *bhakti* is more important than caste or the specific of religion by eating the *ber* fruits first tasted in the forest by the tribal woman Sabari. The Jatayu episode is recalled to emphasise the virtue of gratitude and the lesson is drawn that gratitude in heroes is important for a nation to sustain itself. Sri Rama is depicted here as the ideal son, husband, brother, parent and, indeed, the ideal man. Special mention is made of his faithfulness to one woman—Seeta. Thus the special obligation of society towards women and the ideal of man-woman relationship in Indian hagiology is repeatedly highlighted in this pamphlet.

Karna's *sudra* caste and low birth are mentioned in the context of stories of the heroism with which he maintained status and self-respect. The episode about Karna at Bhanumati's wedding when he valiantly fought many kings to save the dignity of a woman, is also told in this booklet. The electorate is told that NTR always idealised and adored Karna and would follow in his footsteps if he was voted to the helm of affairs of the state.

Bhishma who for the sake of his father's happiness took a vow never to marry is shown as a symbol of sacrifice and a man of principle who kept his word against all odds and at the same time devoted himself to the welfare of the nation.

Sri Krishna Devaraya, who ruled over Andhra and Karnataka, is eulogised for his secular attitudes, for his belief that inter-caste marriages are sanctioned by Dharma, and for his religious tolerance. Although a Vaishnavaite, he built a Saivite temple and helped to re-establish a Muslim kingdom. His services to the Telugu language, poetry and literature and as a patron of scholars are remembered. Also he is remembered for his concern for women—the shelter he gave to fallen women and for his giving court dancers equal status with the women of the royal family. We are told that "in his reign people were religious, patriotic, women secure, the poor farmer free from exploitation, the poets at the height of their creativity. Thus he ruled Telugu Land." The electorate is told that NTR has tried to incorporate the quintessence of Sri Krishna Devaraya's character into his own life.

Brahma Nayadu's attempts to establish a casteless democracy is eulogised too. Similarly, Veera Bramendra Swamy's dedicated work to bring down conflicts between Hindus and Muslims and between castes is praised. We are told that the Swamy was a "favourite of the Muslim rulers." The saint's kindly concern for women is underlined—that he thought that all the ornaments worn by a women are natural to women and should not be removed after the death of her husband, and that he had requested his wife not to stop wearing the *bindi* on her forehead and the bangles when he went into *samadhi*.

Thus, in recalling these loved figures from the cultural heritage, the message components of the Telugu Desam Party to the electorate reiterate certain themes. The protective attitude which the benevolent government have towards women, a government that rises above caste and communal prejudices, a government which upholds democratic principles and, most important of all, a government which is alert to the needs and welfare of the poor. In fact the party manifesto presents precisely these ideals pulled out of India's ancient heritage in 29 detailed points which are operational in today's context.

What is of analytic importance is that the Telugu Desam Party conveys all these leftist and radical principles through home-grown imageries and idioms available in the backyard of the nation.

Pressures of radicalism are inevitable in the context of the following three features of the Indian situation today. First is the elitist socio-economic policies pursued by the Congress governments during the last so many decades. This is evident from the priorities in the fields of education—emphasis on higher education as opposed to universal primary and basic education, and health services—emphasis on individual health such as institutes of medical sciences and hospitals as opposed to public health such as drinking water, sewerage and so on. This is further evident in the massive investments in high technology benefiting those who are in a position to absorb this technology, namely, those who possess capital both in the urban and the rural areas. Consistent with these elitist priorities there has been very little attention paid to the welfare programmes benefiting the masses.

Secondly, the centre-state distribution of financial resources has been such that it has become impossible for the state governments to fulfil their essential political and civic functions. While most of the buoyant sources of revenue are in the hands of the centre, the states are left to tap the resource bases which are both inelastic and politically sensitive to exploit (such as the agricultural sector). States are also charged with functions—education, health, housing, land-reforms, and so on, which most intimately reflect the urgent and fast growing aspirations of the people. Non-performance in these areas obviously has serious consequences.

Thirdly, the elitist socio-economic structure is in inflammatory combination with permissive politics. Undoubtedly, India enjoys a degree of political freedom, and freedom of expression which is rare in most third-world countries. These three features of the Indian situation have created conditions for regionalism as natural as the gravity flow of water.[3]

I may also mention here NTR's statement soon after winning the election that, although he preferred to play the role of Sri Rama—characterizing the ideal man in the film world—in politics he would prefer to play the role of Sri Krishna, the astute and sagacious who restores order in society by destroying the evil and the unjust. Through his cinematic roles Rama Rao has imbibed the complex political manoeuvrings which are available in mythologies, the mythologies which never fail to fascinate the people of India.

At moments of crisis NTR invariably speaks to the people in terms of imageries drawn from the mythologies. The symbol system he uses is redolent with meanings which immediately evoke powerful emotional response from the people. Moreover, it is a symbol system that enable the communication of vast transcendental moralities with maximum economy in words. A good example is his speech during the state government employees strike in July-August 1983 hitting out at Sakunis, Chanakyas and Sukracharyas in the party and the government. In Indian mythology these figures[4] refer to those who seem outwardly to be well-wishers but in reality machinate to bring ruin to those whom they advise. In evoking these legendary figures in the memory-bank of the people, NTR skilfully issued a warning to those concerned without mentioning any names.[5]

The edge that NTR has over veteran political leaders lies in his presentation of issues and problems in terms which are meaningful to the people. The vast masses of the people of India are not literate but they are extremely knowledgeable about their cultural heritage through the oral tradition. NTR has become a winner by appealing through these traditions.[6] Two-thirds of the population of the state being illiterate (64%), it is not surprising that the emotional response of the people to the westernised social-background and jargon of the socialist and communist parties (who should be the logical alternative to the Congress) is not warm. Thus it is that NTR not merely dismantled the ruling Congress, but for good measure also wiped out the opposition parties in the January 1983 election.

Notes and References

1. See in particular, Amal Ray, From consensus to confrontation: Federal politics in India, in *Economic and Political Weekly*, Vol. XVII, No. 40, Oct. 2, 1982, pp. 1619-1623 and his book, *Federal Politics and Government*, Macmillan, Delhi, 1979.
2. *India Today*, Vol. VIII, No. 1, January 1983, p. 25.
3. It is significant that on 4 March when NTR was in Gudivada he said that the state had no powers to decide the annual plan of economic development for itself and that there was no scope for bringing to fruition "our economic ideas". He said further that "We do not have any powers except to say *that the State is ours*". Quoted in the Editorial in *The Deccan Chronicle*, 5 March, 1983.
4. In the *Mahabharata* Duryodhana had imprisoned Sakuni, his brothers and his father. All of them were starved to death except Sakuni. Sakuni took revenge by gaining Duryodhana's confidence by playing on his weakness and giving him wrong advice which ultimately ruined the entire Kaurava dynasty. Sukracharya was the counsellor for the *rakshasas* (demons). Considered a brilliant scholar, he was always competing with Brihaspati—the counsellor for the *devatas* (the gods) even to the point of jeopardising the welfare of the *rakshasas*. Chanakya, an erudite Brahmin was Chandragupta Maurya's advisor and was the author of *Artha*

Sastra (a treatise on political administration). He had been slighted and insulted by the Nandas (the dynasty which was ruling Pataliputra prior to Chandragupta) and avenged himself by helping Chandragupta Maurya to overthrow the Nanda dynasty.

5. The allegation is that some of the senior civil servants alienated the Telugu Desam Party from government employees by rushing into various disciplinary measures (such as the closure of the Secretariat canteens except for the lunch of half hour) without prior dialogue with the people. Besides the "Secretariat Sukracharyas" there are the Sakunis and Chanakyas among party workers—those who intrigue to bring about tension between NTR and his senior colleagues or those who in the name of educating the people isolated the party from the electorate. See *The Deccan Chronicle* report on July 26, 1983.
6. See in this context Professor M.N. Srinivas, Karnataka Elections: Emerging indigenous radicalism? *The Indian Express*, March 10, 1983.

8

A STUDY OF LINKAGES BETWEEN ENVIRONMENT, ELECTORAL PROCESS AND FEDERALISM

AMAL RAY

IN ELECTION studies voting behaviour is not generally related to environmental changes which have occurred over a period of time. The immediate environment is taken note of, and its social and political directions at the time of a particular election, are focussed. Therefore, the temporal dimensions of voting behaviour and their linkages with environmental dynamics are only inadequately perceived. Elections take place at different points of time; these occur under dissimilar environmental situations. Since the first general elections the environment has changed enormously, and has served to breed several important issues which demand depth attention. These issues are: how the evolution of India's political economy has been influencing voting behaviour; in what way and to what extent the elections have or have not been changing the sharing of power among various interest and pressure groups; what political principles of durable value have been highlighted by the elections; and how the elections have been shaping the development of India's polity.

ENVIRONMENTAL SETTING

This paper seeks to describe some of the environmental factors which have shaped 1983 elections in Karnataka and Andhra Pradesh; and secondly, to analyse the elections in terms of their possible effects on federal politics and development process. In terms of voting behaviour and overall consequences the first-three elections exhibited a remarkable thread of unity. All these elections were characterised by ascendancy of the Congress party in both central and state legislatures. A large segment of the electorate was drawn from the people who had seen the role of the Congress in the freedom movement. Again, during this period the village community had not changed much; the traditional authority structure had not been severely undermined. All this served to dilute the democratic principle of responsibility and to breed a feeling of helplessness among the opposition parties.

However, from the middle of the sixties a number of important changes took place in the social, economic and political environment. There arose on the scene a large number of young voters who had seen the Congress party's non-performance, particularly on the issue of the promised social revolution. As the ruling party increasingly displayed its incapacity to fulfil its electoral pledges for important social change and the eradication of poverty, the youth started seriously considering the scope for alternatives. At the same time, Ram Manohar Lohia was making gallant efforts to forge opposition unity on the basis of anti-Congressism. This served to satisfy the longing of a large segment of the electorate for political alternatives. In the mean time the combination of electoral politics and development process was having an upsetting effect on the village community structure. This set in motion two important tendencies. Firstly, the isolation of village economy which was being increasingly eroded during the colonial days, has now virtually been terminated and various spatial levels of India's political economy have been linked together. Secondly, in the wake of massive development investments various interest groups have been politically mobilised and thus has ensued a fierce inter-group competition and scramble for spoils of development.

An equally interesting development is the capitalist mode of production in agriculture in several parts of the country. This has led, on the one hand, to increasing disparities in income and wealth in the countryside and, on the other, rise of a large number of agricultural labourers. This has happened not because of any important structural change in Indian economy, but mainly because of leasing-out of land by a large number of marginal farmers and their joining the ranks of agricultural labourers. This process has broadly been mutually convenient to big farmers and the marginal farmers. While the capitalist farmers have been able to avail of economies of scale, the marginal farmers have enhanced their income as agricultural wage has increased in the wake of green revolution and practice of capitalist mode of production. At the same time, disparities in rural incomes have increased, and consequently, there has been augmentation of rural discontent. However, since the traditional community structure is no longer there in its old rigour and intensity and since no mobilisation maximising political framework has emerged in the countryside, there is no organised rebellion on the part of the disadvantaged to give an articulate expression to their dissatisfaction. The result is that while on the one hand the principle of accountability has come to permeate electoral politics, there has, on the other, arisen a reformist view of development. And this in turn has led to wider distribution of patronage. The greatest constraint on practice of new style of politics is enormous scarcity of resources which puts severe limits to satisfaction of numerous group demands.

ELECTIONS

Now we can place within the aforesaid setting the recently held Karnataka and Andhra Pradesh elections. While in Karnataka misgovernment by Gundu Rao and his men was the principal issue, the issues stirred by the elections in Andhra Pradesh covered in addition the region's cultural heritage and pride, and the centre-state relations. The then chief minister Gundu Rao's authoritarian style of functioning and his government's failure to solve the burning issues of the day, particularly relating to language and the farmers' agitation cost the Congress(I) a large chunk of its traditional votes. The Gokak report, which favoured Kannada as the sole first language, had become an emotional issue in several districts, particularly in old Mysore and Dharwar. Similarly, in these districts farmers associations were well organised and managed to alienate a segment of the rural masses from the ruling party. In old Mysore and some parts of Bombay-Karnataka region the language movement and the farmers' agitation coincided.

Again, while Gundu Rao's style of functioning served to generate simmering discontent in the ruling party, his excessive dependence on the bureaucracy for implementing developmental programmes, particularly in the countryside, served to alienate a number of traditional vote managers. The farmers' agitation was both a reflection and an extension of this alienation process. The dissident activity inside the Karnataka Congress(I) and dissatisfaction among the big and medium-sized farmers combined together to give a blow to the traditional fortress of the ruling party.

Even then the opposition in Karnataka did not expect much. The victory took them by surprise. As Ramakrishna Hegde said : "Till a week before the poll I thought we would never make it. Then I sensed the change in the electorate's mood, and knew that we had a good chance". Besides, their inadequate command over resources had a certain dampening effect upon their campaign. Notwithstanding initial pessimism, the overall outcome of the election went in their favour. The Janata-Ranga coalition obtained 95 seats in a 224-member Assembly. The Congress(I) had to be satisfied with a smaller figure of 81 seats. The Bharatiya Janata Party could secure an impressive number of 18 seats. The Communist Party of India and the Communist Party of India (Marxist) also got some seats. Altogether 23 Independents were returned to the Assembly.

The district-wise distribution of votes would show that the Janata gain came from Bangalore, Chitradurga, Hassan, Shimoga, North Kanara and Chikmagalur, while the Congress majority came from Raichur, Belgaum, Gulbarga, Dharwar, Bidar, Kodagu, Kolar, Bijapur, Bellary. Almost equal strength from both of them was registered from Mysore,

Mandya, and Tumkur. The BJP's maximum gain came from South Kanara. The following Table 8.1 is given to indicate the district-wise pattern of voting.

From Table 8.1 it appears that the Janata gained mostly in Bangalore, Shimoga, Chitradurga, Chikmagalur and North Kanara. This reflects partly the middle class discontent against the authoritarian style of functioning of the Congress(I) leadership at both national and state levels, partly the alienation of the rural leadership from the ruling party, and partly the organisational strength of the Janata Party in some areas of the state. In Bangalore City the Congress(I) lost all the 15 seats it contested. In the dissolved House it had 9 seats from the city. A myriad of factors, mostly locally relevant, played an important role in securing important gains for the Janata. In addition, a certain loss of Muslim support following the breakdown of negotiations between the ruling party and the Indian Union Muslim League and a certain backward community mobilisation led by the Kranti Ranga leader S. Bangarappa had also their roles. The Congress could bag only two of the 11 seats in Chitradurga where Muslims have sizeable share of the population. Similarly, the virtual collapse of the Congress(I) organisation in Shimoga could be attributed to the farmers' agitation.

Most of the BJP gains came from South Kanara. Not only the number of seats, but also, as Table 8.1 shows, the percentage of votes in this district was quite impressive for the BJP. The Congress gains were most spectacular in Hyderabad-Karnataka region. In districts such as Kolar and Bijapur also the Congress made impressive gains.

In Andhra Pradesh the election issues centred around both local corruption and misgovernment and the prime minister's style of functioning. The Telugu Desam emphasised the point again and again that New Delhi, by foisting chief ministers at its own will and without trying to elicit the active wills of the local population, was virtually trampling upon the 'self-respect of the Telugu People'. N.T. Rama Rao built up an extremely efficient publicity and communication system to convince the voters even in remote villages that a two-year period had seen four chief ministers and the Congress(I) president had been changed five times in 30 months. The message which he carried

TABLE 8.1 : **Karnataka assembly elections (January 1983)**

Districts	% of total votes polled	% of invalid votes	% of votes polled				Seats won							
							Cong.(I)		JNP		BJP		Ind	
			Cong.(I)	JNP	BJP	Ind.	S	W	S	W	S	W	S	W
Bangalore	65.90	1.80	35.33	50.33	7.07	7.26	25	3	25	22	16	—	12	—
Bellary	64.23	3.02	42.77	35.71	3.26	18.26	9	5	7	4	3	—	10	—
Belgaum	65.21	9.40	38.66	30.98	2.63	27.34	18	8	17	5	9	—	17	5
Bidar	61.58	2.25	38.58	26.24	16.91	17.97	5	4	6	1	3	1	4	—
Bijapur	64.30	1.86	45.42	25.63	10.35	16.22	15	9	11	3	5	2	14	1
Chikmagalur	64.04	1.97	39 80	46.26	1.59	12.35	5	1	5	4	3	—	5	—
Chitradurga	70.58	2.29	41.12	47.79	2.83	7.90	11	4	10	7	—	—	—	—
Dharwar	68.16	3.05	39.87	28.95	8.30	22.80	18	7	15	6	6	1	18	4
Gulbarga	54.45	4.20	40.06	36.12	10.19	13.13	13	5	13	7	7	1	11	—
Hassan	69.20	1.76	37.65	39.19	10.60	12.17	7	3	7	5	5	—	10	—
Kodagu	62.12	0.97	41.84	19.50	16.99	21.96	3	2	2	1	2	—	3	—
Kolar	72.56	2.08	41.68	21.12	—	33.83	5	5	5	3	1	—	13	4
Mysore	55.24	2.60	34.43	34.29	10.00	21.27	15	5	16	8	12	1	14	2
Mandya	76.01	1.92	42.97	40.43	1.85	14.30	9	4	9	4	2	—	8	1
Uttara Kannada	62.17	2 35	31.80	39.92	15.75	12.13	6	2	5	3	4	1	6	—
Raichur	51.28	4.64	51.10	17.87	9.44	18.59	11	8	7	1	4	—	7	2
Shimoga	73.00	2,83	31.11	40.63	16.90	11.08	10	1	10	6	6	2	11	1
Dakshina Kannada	66.27	1.44	39.40	21.50	29 38	9.70	15	3	11	4	11	8	11	—
Tumkur	68 45	2.16	36 53	33.85	7.82	21.14	13	2	12	1	5	1	32	4

Notes : S=Seats contested.
W=Seats won.
Ind : includes Maharashtra Ekikarana Samiti (MES).

effectively with the people was that no Telugu government worth the name could function independently and honestly unless it could uphold the dignity and self-respect of the Telugu people against assaults by the centre. This, as the election manifesto of his party emphasised, necessitated a minimal federation. Hence, the state government should possess all decision-making powers except defence, foreign affairs, currency and communication "which should be under the purview of the Central Government".

In the elections Telugu Desam had a colossal victory. The Congress lost heavily in coastal Andhra and Rayalaseema. Table 8.2 is likely to provide an insight into the newly emergent correlation of political forces in Andhra Pradesh.

An analysis of voting pattern in Andhra Pradesh shows that the Congress(I) suffered heavily in coastal Andhra and Rayalaseema. It is further seen that although the Congress(I) party's performance in Telangana region was good, it lost heavily in the urban areas. For instance, the party failed to secure even one seat in Hyderabad city. It is thus found that the people in both coastal Andhra and Rayalaseema and the urbanites in general voted against the ruling party. Thus the voting behaviour in Andhra Pradesh shows a combination of several factors. The Kammas in particular and the prosperous peasantry in general revolted against the Congress(I). This in part reflects the caste loyalty of the Kammas for Rama Rao and partly represents the protest of the rural elites against some or all of the central and/or state policies on agricultural development. In Rayalaseema the swing in favour of Telugu Desam revealed an eloquent protest of the people amidst caste fissures against long neglect of their interests by successive Congress(I) governments. The urban revolt symbolised their resistance to superimposition of central mores and patterns upon the state politics and government. However, more importantly the Andhra election results exhibited a rare display of primordial attachments of the Telugu people.

TABLE 8.2 : **Andhra Pradesh assembly election (January 1983)**

Districts	% of total votes polled	% of invalid votes	% of votes polled						
			Cong.	TDP	Ind.	Janata	CPM	BJP	Others
(1)	(2)	(3)	(4)	(5)	(6)	(7)	(8)	(9)	(10)
Anantapur	68.63	2.11	30.26	55.02	9.99	0.12	2.18	0.32	—
Adilabad	64.52	3.64	37.96	30.16	14.79	2.19	6.92	4.34	—
Chittor	74.43	1.73	40.41	50.53	6.80	0.09	—	0.44	—
Cuddapah	74.99	1.48	32.69	53.35	12.04	—	0.34	0.10	—
East Godavari	71.30	1.00	26.53	60.78	10.81	0.06	0.12	0.16	—
Guntur	64.99	1.69	29.61	60.35	2.97	0.05	4.01	1 32	—
Hyderabad	58.16	2.09	20.87	27.06	5.73	1.20	1.07	20.83	21.78
Karimnagar	60.14	2.92	31.15	41.20	15.54	0.06	5.97	3.16	—
Khammam	71.02	1.77	34.68	25.29	7.11	—	30.96	0.19	—
Krishna	71.97	1.33	25.66	32.82	13.19	1.00	25.89	0.11	—
Kurnool	69.02	2.29	44.85	48.12	3.37	0.09	0.77	0.51	—
Medak	69.63	2.20	44.20	28.88	15.39	—	4.39	4.94	—
Mehboobnagar	82.66	2.37	41.92	35.28	8.88	7.84	—	3.71	—
Nalgonda	69.27	1.63	35.46	27.51	9.22	0.05	23.86	2.27	—
Nizamabad	68.91	3 02	31.66	46.44	15.64	0.33	—	2.91	—
Nellore	67.42	2.97	31.39	53.03	3.07	1.23	5.01	6.00	—
Prakasam	69.26	1.61	34.65	51.09	6.12	1.36	4.72	0.45	—
Rangareddy	68.67	2.68	43.25	22.57	25.99	—	5.24	1.37	—

TABLE 8.2—*contd.*

(1)	(2)	(3)	(4)	(5)	(6)	(7)	(8)	(9)	(10)
Srikakulam	72.57	2.39	30.32	49.68	15.49	0.30	1.82	—	—
Visakhapatnam	61.42	2.46	27.15	57.36	8.68	0.83	1.82	1.70	—
Vizianagaram	73.50	2.42	29.58	53.42	12.57	—	1.13	0.88	—
Warangal	69.67	2.41	40.02	29.21	3.82	1.35	9.25	13.94	—
West Godavari	68.21	1.42	23.32	62.84	7.64	1.82	2.82	0.14	—

Note : S=Seats contested.
W=Seats won.

TABLE 8.2—*contd.*

Districts	Seats won													
	Cong. (I)		TDP		Ind.		Janata		CPM*		BJP		Others	
	S	W	S	W	S	W	S	W	S	W	S	W	S	W
(1)	(11)	(12)	(13)	(14)	(15)	(16)	(17)	(18)	(19)	(20)	(21)	(22)	(23)	(24)
Anantapur	14	1	14	12	9	1	2	0	2	0	1	0	—	—
Adilabad	9	4	7	4	7	1	3	0	2	0	3	0	—	—
Chittor	15	0	15	14	13	1	1	0	0	0	3	0	—	—
Cuddapah	11	4	11	6	11	1	4	0	10	0	3	0	—	—
East Godavari	21	0	21	21	20	0	6	0	10	0	6	0	—	—
Guntur	19	1	19	18	17	0	1	0	7	0	8	0	—	—
Hyderabad	13	0	13	7	12	0	10	0	2	0	13	1	5	5
Karimnagar	13	6	13	7	13	0	1	0	4	0	5	0	—	—
Khammam	8	3	9	1	8	0	—	—	8	5	1	0	—	—
Krishna	17	4	17	12	16	1	3	0	6	0	2	0	—	—
Kurnool	13	4	13	9	9	0	1	0	1	0	1	0	—	—
Medak	10	6	10	3	9	1	—	—	1	0	3	0	—	—
Mehboobnagar	13	6	13	6	13	1	8	0	—	—	3	0	—	—
Nalgonda	12	5	12	4	10	2	1	0	9	1	4	0	—	—
Nizamabad	8	2	9	7	9	0	—	—	—	—	6	0	—	—
Nellore	11	1	11	10	1	0	3	0	8	0	1	0	—	—
Prakasam	13	0	13	12	9	1	1	0	4	0	2	0	—	—
Rangareddy	6	3	6	0	6	3	5	0	5	0	0	0	—	—

	(11)	(12)	(13)	(14)	(15)	(16)	(17)	(18)	(19)	(20)	(21)	(22)	(23)	(24)
Srikakulam	12	1	12	11	12	0	2	0	3	0	—	—	—	—
Vishakhapatnam	15	1	15	13	13	1	2	0	2	0	7	0	—	—
Vizianagaram	10	1	9	8	6	1	—	—	2	0	1	0	—	—
Warangal	13	7	13	4	12	0	2	0	7	1	8	1	—	—
West Godavari	16	0	16	15	15	1	4	0	5	0	2	0	—	—

*CPI/CPM.

OUTLOOK FOR FEDERALISM

It is now possible to discuss a certain similarity in voting behaviour in both Karnataka and Andhra Pradesh. Firstly, in both the states the middle class exhibited an enormous antipathy towards the ruling party. Both in Bangalore and Hyderabad cities the Congress(I) could not obtain even a single seat. Secondly, the ruling party suffered enormously in culturally homogeneous regions in both Karnataka and Andhra Pradesh. While the Telugu Desam's performance was best in Coastal Andhra which might be called the seat of Telugu culture, the Janata-Kranti Ranga's electoral success was most spectacular in Old Mysore region which may be called the citadel of Kannada culture and civilisation. The revolt of the voters in these regions might symbolise an earnest desire on their part to protect their distinctive cultural personalities against a powerful tendency in recent years towards standardisations.

A connected event which is equally interesting is that the Congress(I) fared very well in culturally traditional areas. For instance, the Congress party got 17 seats and 42 seats in Hyderabad-Karnataka and Telangana regions respectively. In both the regions the record of Janata-Kranti Ranga combine and Telugu Desam was most unimpressive.

The combination of urban protest with rural revolt in culturally homogeneous regions in both Karnataka and Andhra Pradesh provides an important base for generating demands against New Delhi. Added to this is the support extended to both Janata and Telugu Desam by farmer lobbies. Lately, a certain conflict of interests between the national bourgeois and the rural elites has been discernible. This seems to have impelled the latter to come close to the local parties in order that their interests might be espoused by them. Of course, the situation in Andhra Pradesh is largely different from that in Karnataka. The anti-centre impulse is rooted deeply in the electoral process and voting behaviour in the former state. N.T. Rama Rao's principal election plank was based on an appeal to the past and a crusading zeal to restore the glory of the Telugus. He emphasised again and again that New Delhi and its Telugu representatives were responsible for loss of self-respect of the Telugu people. His call for an indigenous government in tune with local culture and genius carried conviction with the Telugu people.

Notwithstanding the deep regional roots of the voting behaviour in Andhra Pradesh, it appears that Karnataka has been exhibiting greater capacity for generating and mobilising regional demands for a relatively balanced federation. Partly this reflects the strategy of Hegde government to stir up a high-level political mobilisation in order to cover up its numerical weaknesses in the state legislature. Partly also this represents an earnest desire to mitigate the structural constraints which stand in the way of the state government's effective performance in their constitutionally allotted areas. All this is sought to be accomplished by organising the non-Congress(I) state governments for the necessary changes in the ordering framework of India's federation. Ramakrishna Hegde being a person of remarkable political acumen and experience, could perceive that a meaningful beginning could be made by mobilising the southern states for this purpose. Sometime in March four southern Chief Ministers of Tamil Nadu, Andhra Pradesh, Pondicherry and Karnataka, belonging to different non-Congress(I) parties, met in Bangalore and founded a forum for tackling their common problems and for seeking drastic changes in centre-state relations, particularly in the fiscal area.

All these chief ministers, who addressed a joint news conference on 20 March, made it clear that the forum christened "the Council of the Chief Ministers of the Southern States" was intended to promote the concept of co-operative federalism between the states and the centre. A strong centre, they said, was as much necessary as strong states. An important consensus recommendation of the council was that the centre should appoint a fiscal commission, with adequate representation for the states and statutory powers, to review centre-state fiscal relations in the light of the experience of states over the last thirty-five years. The commission, they emphasised, should recommend amendments to the Constitution and enactments for a more equitable distribution of resources between the centre and the states.

The conference pinpointed a wide spectrum of constitutional provisions requiring re-examination in its view. These were administrative relations under Articles 256 and 257 of the Constitution and legislative powers, including redrafting of the seventh Schedule to the Constitution. Also the conference emphasised that the legislature should have powers to enact laws in the state list and the concurrent list (when states are the first to legislate on the subject), without the need to get the President's assent. It was further said that the independence and competence of judiciary should be safeguarded by ensuring that high court judges are familiar with the language of the states concerned.

This meeting of the southern chief ministers held at the initiative of the Karnataka chief minister came to be regarded as an extremely significant event. When these chief ministers were later supported by other non-Congress(I) chief ministers for changes in the federal structure of the Indian Constitution, an enormous pressure was created for the prime minister to set up a commission to review centre-state relation. The temper of the Bangalore conclave was later carried to Vijayawada where a larger congregation of non-Congress(I) political leaders and chief ministers reiterated the earlier demand and gave a clarion call for united resistance to prime minister's style of functioning and her persistent effort to superimpose upon India's federalising processes a system of uniformities and standardisations.

A depth view of recent developments in Indian politics and government would further show that the new governments in south India, particularly the Government of Karnataka are increasingly becoming centres of new impulses in development, planning and administration. Immediately on assumption of office the Hegde government set up a new institution called Social and Economic Council. It is a top level expert committee with its membership drawn from various discipline and different parts of the country, intended to advise the government on developmental and administrative matters. It appears that this committee is playing a significant role in enhancing the quality of planning and administration in Karnataka. This has already influenced the thinking of the central leaders who have set up almost a similar institution called Economists' Council.

It is further seen that the Hegde government is trying to bring down the federalising process to grassroots level. For them the demand for a balanced federation is actually a part of the movement for decentralisation. The government's current move to restructure the existing Panchayati Raj system and to set up a new elected and powerful tier at the district level reflects their commitment to culture of decentralisation and participatory rural development. Thus when the Hegde government fight for state autonomy, it is only a part of their battle for a really decentralised polity.

CONCLUSION

However, the installation in power of Telugu Desam and Janata Party in Andhra Pradesh and Karnataka respectively is, however, both a promise and a warning. It is a promise in the sense it marks an eloquent protest against illegitimate central encroachments on regional autonomy and an ardent will to map out a new route to development. At the same time, the assumption of power by Telugu Desam and the Janata Party is a warning in the sense an excess of localism might ultimately be disruptive of India's national unity. The danger of balkanisation is inherent in India's federal society where linguistic and cultural particularisms have a highly explosive potential, especially when these operate in an extremely resource scarce economy. What has recently been happening in some parts of the country, especially in Assam and Punjab, points to this danger. If the recent drift to local politics in south India is pushed too far, it may generate powerful tendencies in the direction of loosening the fabric of India's "unity in diversity". Already, some such tendencies have been surfacing out. The powerfully manifest primordial attachments to language in both Karnataka and Andhra Pradesh and the middle class job hunters' bid to localise employment market, are instances to the point. So the challenge before the non-Congress(I) governments is not to evolve a Bangladesh model of regional autonomy, but to formulate a model of development where the states are not hindered by power or resource inadequacy to evolve autonomous impulses, programmes and strategies of development in their constitutionally allotted areas and at the same time, the nexus of India's composite culture and national interests is not imperilled. This is extremely significant in the contemporary situation of India's dangerously pluralising politics. A plural society having abiding roots in linguistic, religious and caste particularisms, has been involved in a process of change and development. Consequently, the particularistic groups are increasingly becoming politically mobilised. At the same time, because of enormous scarcity of resources it is not possible even for the most generous governments to fulfil all the patronage demands. This has led to a certain disenchantment with the existing governmental system and has encouraged the newly mobilised groups to take recourse to extra-constitutional militant actions. These symbolise inner strains and stresses of a plural society undergoing a critical pluralising process.

9

POPULAR PRESSURE FOR A NORMATIVE CHANGE IN POLITICS

BASHIRUDDIN AHMED

THE INDIAN electorate is no longer quiescent as it was in the first fifteen years of electoral politics. It has over the years become an active element in our politics, playing the role that citizens as voters are assigned in democratic politics: to choose their rulers and hold them accountable for what they do or fail to do when in office. The electorate's ability to play this role effectively is crucial to the proper functioning of a democratic system. If the electorate fails in its role there is no other element in the system that could step in and take its place. In such an event the accountability mechanism of the system ceases to operate, elections turn into rituals, and the representative character of the elected governments becomes a farce.

As the results of the January 1983 elections to the state assemblies in Andhra Pradesh and Karnataka show, we have fortunately been spared such a fate. By now there is enough evidence to show that the electorate has consistently put into practice the accountability principle in election after election, ever since the 1967 elections. That was the year when the electorate for the first time showed that its support could not be taken for granted; that no party, not even the Congress which had brought freedom to the country, had any title to rule except on the basis of its record in office.

The economic conditions in the country, it will be recalled, were extremely bad in 1967, following three successive droughts, an industrial recession and a severe inflation. The electorate held the ruling party responsible for these conditions and pushed it out of power in eight states, and drastically reduced its impressive majority in the Parliament from 75 per cent of the seats to an all time low of 54 per cent.

In the intervening period between the Fourth (1967) and the Fifth General Elections (1971), however, the economic situation had improved. A string of successful monsoons and the government-initiated agricultural programmes contributed to the 'Green Revolution', altering the gloomy economic picture to one of considerable hope. Acute shortages were over, the prices climbed down and industrial production picked up, ending the long period of recession. But even as the economic situation improved, inter-party strife and governmental instability appeared in most of the states where coalition governments had taken over from the Congress in 1967. Instead of improving upon the record of Congress governments they had replaced, their record in office was characterised, for the most part, by petty squabbles, inaction, and lack of movement forward. The occurrence of widespread violence and lawlessness in some of these states only made an already bad situation look even worse. If before the Fourth General Election the bad economic conditions in the country were a source of public unhappiness and discontent, in the period before the Fifth General Election the failure of the coalition governments to function effectively became the source of public disenchantment.

While the changing economic and political situation helped considerably in reducing the anti-Congress feelings that had resulted in a major set-back for the Congress in 1967, the split in the party in 1969 did much more. It generated strong and positive sentiments in the country for the ruling group under Indira Gandhi. The split provided Indira Gandhi and her supporters with an opportunity to play the role of counter-elite, standing for structural change, while the "Syndicate" and its supporters were cast in the public eye as defenders of the interests and privileges of the rich, and as promoters of a style of politics in which party machine, middlemen, patronage and corruption thrived to the total neglect of public interest.

An equally powerful theme emphasised by Indira Gandhi's new Congress in 1971 campaign was that of political stability and a strong and effective government. With the record of ineffectiveness in office of non-Congress coalition governments in several states providing the backdrop, the need for stability gained an added importance when Indira Gandhi's government was reduced to a minority government following the 1969 split in the Congress Party. The danger of instability at the centre became real for the first time, giving cause for worry to those concerned about the survival of the system itself. With the Old Congress projected as the main obstacle to radical socio-economic change and most of the opposition in the dock for the mess in the state, the new Congress swept to victory in the 1971 elections. The sweep was complete. It covered all parts of the country enabling the new Congress to boost its strength in the Lok Sabha from 228 at the time of the dissolution of the House to 350.

If after the 1967 elections there were still any doubts about the character of the electorate's response to the performance factor they were convincingly allayed by the outcome of the 1971 elections. The elections demonstrated in no uncertain terms that the electorate was not a docile and malleable collectivity whose responses could be shaped by party bosses and middlemen, dominant castes, or local notables. Instead, the results highlighted once again the new assertiveness of the electorate and its capacity to engage both in reprisal and reward under appropriate circumstances.

It was indeed this twice demonstrated capacity that was responsible for the massive defeat of the ruling Congress party in 1977 elections, and, again, that of the ruling Janata party in 1980. Significantly, there were no specific economic factors in 1977, or in 1980, to explain the humiliating failure the incumbents suffered in these two elections. The electorate's disapproval and anger on both occasions had obviously had some other basis. Both the results, it seems to me, were a reflection of a marked sensitivity in significant sections of the electorate, to negative aspects of elite political culture. In throwing out first the Congress and then the Janata, the voters it would appear, were reacting as much to the style of politics marked by self-aggrandizement and hubris of the politicians, their unprincipled struggles for office and group advantage, and their rampant corruption and factionalism, as to the end products of this style characterised by endemic instability and manipulative politics, instead of effective governance and purposive action desired by the people.

Similar sentiments appear to have operated in the Andhra and Karnataka assembly elections also. Large sections of the electorate turned away from the Congress(I) in these two states more for reasons of political culture than for economic or other reasons.

As other papers in this volume indicate, a range of state-specific social and economic factors were indeed there in the elections in these two states, but they seem to have been closely interlocked with widespread public unhappiness over matters of political culture. The themes stressed in the manifesto of the Telugu Desam Party highlight this linkage well. In Karnataka, too, the defeat of the Congress(I) appears to owe as much to the correct arithmetic of the caste coalition the Janata-Kranti Ranga combine put together, as to the political style of Gundu Rao and the shenanigans of other Congress(I) luminaries and legislators in the state.

This is an aspect of the electoral dynamics which has not received the attention it deserves. Neither the observers of the Indian political scene, nor the active participants in our politics, seem to have fully grasped the significance of this new factor influencing the electoral outcome. The Congress(I), it seems, overlooked it. It presumably proceeded on the assumption that the electorate operates only according to the calculus of caste interests or material gains and losses. Thus, if the prices are not rising, the essential commodities are not in short supply, and the claims of various social groups have been met through appropriate distribution of party tickets, the ruling party can pretty much count on cornering a winning percentage of votes irrespective of its style of politics. The voters in Andhra and Karnataka showed, as the voters in the country had shown earlier in 1977 and 1980, that this is not a safe assumption to make.

To say this, however, is not to suggest that other social and economic factors do not influence the electoral outcomes. The point rather is that they do not adequately account for the results of the elections being considered here. Because, while individuals and groups do have social and economic interests which matter a lot to them, they also have a set of social and political values which are not directly tied to or always expressive of their narrow interests or those of the group to which they belong. Such values create for them a realm of social beliefs and orientations which may overlap the realm created by their other interests but which need not be coterminous with it. This fact has a range of consequences for the way individuals and groups respond to situations in their larger environment. Firstly, they tend to react to and take strong positions on events and developments around them even when these do not directly impinge on their well-being or interests. Secondly, their social beliefs and orientations modify the character of their responses in ways not fully consistent with their social affiliation or economic interests.

Looked at in this perspective, the outcomes of the Andhra and Karnataka elections (as well as those of the 1977 and 1980 parliamentary elections) acquire a significance that goes beyond the immediate fact of Congress defeat. They point to the growing salience of issues of political style and culture in our politics independently of other issues. Prevailing socio-economic conditions will, of course, matter but issues of political culture are likely to have an important role in determining electoral outcomes till such time that the style and tenure of our politics change substantially, from what it has been so far, to one in which public purpose, a respect for democratic norms and institutions and probity in public life become the dominant elements.

When it comes to changing the culture of our politics there is not much the voters can do beyond what they have done, namely, throw out the rulers who refuse to change. Ultimately it is the political elite who will make this change possible, provided they read the message of the electoral outcomes correctly. So far it appears that they have not done so, or, if they have, they have not taken the message seriously enough to alter their ways of conducting public affairs. But the context of the Andhra and Karnataka elections was such that there should be no ambiguity about the message of the outcomes there. Translating these messages into appropriate actions, however, will be a matter of opportunity and skill.

In Andhra, N.T. Rama Rao's victory was stupendous, giving him an overwhelming majority in the legislature. This kind of majority should enable him to move in the direction of evolving a new culture and style of politics that the Andhra voters clearly want. But he may not be able to do so, whether for want of ideas or for the lack of requisite political skills. So far, his record in office, has, at best, been mixed. It has been marked more by populism and personalisation of power than care in policy making and concern for norms and institutions. He could well change for the better. There is still time, unless he commits some horrendeous mistakes and gives the centre an opportunity to intervene. But if this does not happen and Rama Rao has a full term without achievements, then he may well have to go when the next elections come. I doubt if the Andhra electorate would continue to support him if he merely reproduces the Congress(I) brand of politics. In fact, in that event the Andhra voters may even turn back to the Congress(I) should a better alternative not be available to them. The Congress(I) is still a significant factor in Andhra. Although it lost heavily in terms of seats, there is considerable popular support for it in the state. While it could only get 60 seats in the Assembly against the 175 it had won in 1978, its votes declined less precipitatiously: from 39.24 per cent to only 33.49 per cent.

In Karnataka, on the other hand, Ramakrishna Hegde has the necessary political acumen and skills to steer the politics of Karnataka in the right direction but he lacks Rama Rao's advantage, viz., a solid majority in the state assembly. He has with him a group of only 133 members in a house of 225. The group is made up of 14 independent MLAs and MLAs affiliated to four other parties besides his own. This puts him in a highly vulnerable position—vulnerable to pressures both from within his coalition as well as from the opposition.

As we prepare this paper for publication, there are indications that despite their respective limitations, both the governments have, in different ways, managed to strengthen the process of evolving a new political culture. In Andhra, this impression is reinforced by the fact that the chief minister's son, N. Jayakrishna, has ultimately forsaken the advantage he had gained earlier by getting a Government Order (GO) that permitted him to use the premises of his family's Ramakrishna cine studio for commercial purposes, even while it was located in a non-commercial zone. That he could get such an order issued by the government had dismayed the public, for the government order was seen as an instance of the chief minister's son using his father's position for self-aggrandizement. Rama Rao, of course, denied that this was the case, but his opponents, the press and the public refused to see things his way. As a result, after months of discussion and comment, public opinion has, as it were, triumphed. Early in December N. Jayakrishna issued a statement "relinquishing", as the press put it, "all the benefits he would have enjoyed if he had availed himself of the Government Order . . ." Jayakrishna's reasons for this act of self-denial are worth noting. They were, as he put it, to protect the "fair name" of his father. "Let not", he added, "the vested interests try to defame my father hereafter using this GO as a convenient handle for their nefarious ends and ulterior designs. . . not the slightest whisper should be heard tarnishing the great name of our leader".[1]

This, of course is a small step. Its significance, however, lies in its reflecting the recognition on the part of the Andhra chief minister and his son of a close nexus between probity in handling private interests of their family and its political costs or gains. This is important, for politicians will be loath to abstain from self-aggrandizement or to engage in principled politics on their own unless they are required to do so by circumstances. The changes of the kind the public wants in the culture of our politics will indeed come about only when the recognition of such a nexus pervades political life.

In Karnataka, the revelations about Congress (I), efforts

to buy MLAs with a view to toppling the Hegde government have galvanised public opinion as never before. Within Karnataka itself public reaction has had the effect of deterring the concerned MLAs from defecting to the Congress(I). Vasant Bangera, the Bharatiya Janata Party MLA who had defected to the Karnataka Kranti Ranga, returned to his party when a negative reaction to his defection developed in his constituency. Two others, G.F. Upnal and Father Jacob, who were reported to have joined the Congress(I), hastily denied that they had done so, following the ill-treatment Hutchmasti Gowda, an independent MLA who had declared his intention to join the Congress(I), was subjected to in Chikmagalur.[2]

There are two things relating to these developments in Karnataka that deserve attention. Hegde's government gained a lease of life which a government as vulnerable as his (in terms of its strength in the assembly) could not have possibly gained in the earlier phase of our politics. This was because Hegde could, in effect, convert the Congress(I)'s attempt to violate norms of good politics into a positive resource for himself. His success also revealed how acting in defence of norms of good politics, given the growing public concern for them can now bring to parties and leaders political gains which in the past they could only have obtained by resort to devious means. Conversely, the Congress(I) attracted a degree of odium which could well prove politically costly to it, especially if it persists in the face of widespread disapproval of its efforts, to topple the Hegde government through defections. Even if it were to succeed in this, the success may well turn out to be pyrrhic.

In placing the outcomes of the Andhra and Karnataka elections alongside those of the last few parliamentary elections, our purpose in this paper has been to suggest that the former are not isolated events produced by factors peculiar to Andhra or Karnataka. Instead they must be viewed as fresh instances of the influence on electoral outcomes of the public's desire for better politics. This desire, we believe, is widespread and likely to persist till it is met in adequate measure by political parties and leaders. What specific directions events will take in the future in Karnataka or

Andhra Pradesh is difficult to say. But, should those elected to office in 1983 succeed in making a palpable difference in the conduct of public affairs in these two states, they would not only get political mileage out of it for themselves but also contribute to the strengthening of public pressure for better politics in the country as a whole.

Notes and References

1. *Hindustan Times*, December 4, 1983.
2. *India Today*, December 15, 1983, pp. 64-72.

10

PRIMORDIALITY IN INDIAN POLITICS
The Case of 1983 Elections in Andhra Pradesh and Karnataka

GEORGE MATHEW

In federalism, different communities may assert their cultural identity and utilise them as vehicles to demand political, economic and social rights. This paper argues that it will not necessarily destroy the national fabric. The first generation of India's political leadership had recognised the positive aspect of India's varied cultural identity (creation of linguistic states). But since late 1960s more centralisation had happened resulting in the neglect of regional feelings on the political, economic as well as cultural levels (e.g. ignoring local political leadership, farmers' demands, language demands). In the 1983 Andhra Pradesh and Karnataka assembly elections, people gave vent to their wounded feelings by overthrowing the party which without honouring the regional sentiments centralised the powers. Taking the cue from the happenings since the election, we argue that regional emphasis can work against centrifugal forces. This questions the validity of the thesis on early years of independent India by scholars like Clifford Geertz who had said that strong primordial sentiments are a threat to its integration; that is, strong primordial feelings and civil society will not go together. In the concluding session we raise doubts about the often quoted charisma of political leaders like Indira Gandhi. As the self awareness and political consciousness increase through primordial identities, people's dependence on charismatic personalities will be diminishing.

Primordial in the literal sense means that which formed earliest or that which is first in order. In sociological literature this is used to identify that which evokes intense and comprehensive solidarity among people. Edward Shils for instance identifies common territory of origin and residence, common place of work, ties of blood and sexual connection as primordial.[1] This has several functional levels in view of the contexts in which it becomes operational. For example, in a village it may be the family and caste, in a province it may be the caste and religion. This paper, in the context of a nation comprising many old societies, is treating primordial to denote linguistic and cultural identities.

India's survival as a unified nation has always been in question. One of the reasons for the apprehension was the fact that the people who were brought together to form the Indian union had age old traditions of culture, rich but varied, and it would result in centrifugal forces having an upper hand resulting in the balkanisation of the country. They had no tradition of political unity as a nation except that imposed by British rule. The formation of Pakistan was considered a portent of what might happen to the rest of the country. Selig S. Harrison had raised the bogey in his book *India : The Most Dangerous Decades*. He quoted two important leaders who had stated that the centrifugal forces would ultimately prevail; therefore India faced the threat of being split into any number of small nationalities.[2] It would need a high level of political skill to keep these cultural groupings within a federal structure. Whether such a skilful leadership would be forthcoming was a question at issue. A landmark in the history of independent India was the restructuring of the constituent states on a linguistic basis. The state units of the Indian National Congress were already organised on linguistic basis but the national leaders did not want to redraw state boundaries until the popular sentiment demanded it. When India recognised the linguistic divisions for the reorganisation of its states, for the first time, political boundaries were crystallising in accordance with the linguistic boundaries recognised by the ruling political party. It set in motion the process for the low-caste masses to activate their socio-cultural dynamism to seek their self-identity in the newly-vitalised regional languages that were firmly entrenched in their historic locations.[3]

But fear of India's political disintegration was present all these years in the subconscious of all concerned. It used to find expression overtly and covertly in different forms; not least of all in the statements by the leaders of the ruling party itself. The threat to national unity and integrity became the major election plank as well as basis for political legitimacy of the ruling party. A dialectical interaction came into play wherein the superstructure of the national regime was continually strengthened even as the different states developed their autonomous identities. However, this dialectical process entered a new stage of its historical development when the country's dominant political party found that it was being challenged in Andhra Pradesh and Karnataka in the 1983 elections by regional parties and regional leadership that carried the potential of transforming the national political authority as well. In short, ominous signs were noted by some political observers in the rising of regional aspirations that portended transformation of the entire Indian polity.

An evaluation of the emerging political scenario is indeed a difficult task. Are national issues more critical than those at the state or local levels? How are the residents of Andhra going to define their political identity and loyalty as between the Indian nation and *Telugu Desam?* Can the local and regional rights of people be subordinated to what may be called the superordinate values like nationalism, national unity and integrity? Can it happen that succumbing to regional loyalties will negate all that we have been building as an Indian nation all these years?

I

Edward Shils has argued that under certain circumstances man is much more concerned with what is present and concrete than with what is remote and abstract. "He is more responsive on the whole to persons, to the status of those who surround him and the justice which he sees in his own situation than he is with the symbols of remote persons, with the total status system in the society and with the global system of justice."[4] What is immediate to him which could evoke intense responses are the so-called "primordial sentiments".

But this argument has another important dimension that is often ignored. As soon as man developed a "mind" or "soul", he needed an abstract world as a self-respecting human being. The need for such a framework of ideas and beliefs constitutes the search for identity. In course of cultural evolution, the search for identity becomes complex and creates its own problems. Politics (as well as economics) become means as well as ends. That is, the ordinary man is not an idiot in the Greek sense. He is not unresponsive to the happenings around him. In some manner, he too responds to the symbols of larger society or the state.[5] As occasion arises his consciousness comprehends the larger issues of society. In other words, it is possible for a state of comprehensive national solidarity to exist independently of or as complementary to the primordial. Either bypassing or encompassing the primordial ties, integration of a larger society can take place. No doubt, there may be differences in the degree of attachments. The attachment to primordiality will usually be more intense, to that of other value systems will be less intense except on special occasions. There is some kind of a "sacredness" attached to the former and hence, if somebody attacks it, it will be violently resisted. In short, primordial attachment, its fervour and passion are not necessarily inimical to the maintenance of a civil society.

This provides some clues in order to grasp what had happened and what is happening in the two states under study *vis-a-vis* the Indian federal structure.

The Congress(I) strategy has become that of 'divide and win' by separating the different strata of population along the lines of caste or religion, to win their support by playing upon the distrust and insecurity among them but offering them security because the party embodies the national and secular authority. This happened on the state level as well as the national, depending upon how it suited the ruling party's interest. In the situation of a state, for instance, every social segment was told that its survival and security depended on the Congress party. By and large, this strategy succeeded until recently in winning votes for the party. But at the subliminal level the tactic created negative consequences in the form of religious groups fighting against one another, ethnic groups ranged against other ethnic or linguistic groups. In this process, the role of the once monolithic Congress party in perpetuating conflicts and keeping the regions in an unbalanced state of economic growth did not receive adequate attention of the regional elites themselves.

The results of the Andhra Pradesh and Karnataka election indicate the success of a counter strategy: winning support of the people on the basis of their solidarity and unity. In Andhra Pradesh particularly the basis of solidarity was language and common culture; a similar social solidarity was evident in Karnataka.[6]

One of the important election planks of the Telugu Desam Party (TDP) led by N.T. Rama Rao was to restore the self-respect of the 60 million Telugu people. His main political slogan was *Telugu atma gowravam* (pride of the Telugu people). *Telugu Desam* means 'Land of the Telugu'. It is unabashedly regional. The posture of TDP indicated that Telugu people's self-respect had been wounded. It had happened at two levels: one the government level, and the other of party politics.

There was a widespread feeling that political affairs in Andhra were being stage managed from Delhi. Within a short period of three years after Indira Gandhi returned to power, Andhra Pradesh had four chief ministers. Chenna Reddy was in power at the time having become chief minister in 1978. He was removed from office in 1980 to be followed by T. Anjaiah, B. Venkatram Reddy and Vijaybhaskar Reddy. To crown it all, T. Anjaiah was publicly humiliated by an important national Congress(I) personality. He had to quit the chief ministership in tears. N.T. Rama Rao characterised the ouster of Anjaiah as an "auctioning of Andhra's honour in Delhi". A chief minister, to whichever party he might belong, symbolises the honour of the people of the state. When he is treated in a contemptuous manner by those in power outside the state, even if they are national leaders, regional feelings rise against the offenders. In Andhra the people supported their humiliated leader with a vengeance. T. Anjaiah was returned in the 1983 election with a huge majority even though the 'wave' against his own Congress(I) party swept the state.

Whittling down the authority of the chief ministers had begun in 1969 when the Congress party split. The split divided the central leadership of the party under Indira Gandhi from the organisational wing led mainly by the old-timers. The latter organised themselves as Organisation Congress or Congress(O) as against the Indira Congress or Congress(I). The latter has ever since then ruled without an adequate organisational party base while the former splintered time and again for the lack of effective leaders. The central leadership of the Congress(I) has relegated the state party units to insignificance. Especially after Indira Gandhi's return to power in 1980, the Congress(I) high command often imposed on the states chief ministers for whom the people of the states had very little regard. Gundu Rao of Karnataka is a case in point. Central domination was also very much evident in the electioneering in 1983. Every detail of the election campaign, starting from selection of candidates, financing, posters and publicity campaigns, was organised from New Delhi. The prime minister visited each and every constituency while ignoring the local leadership. A news magazine reported: "The current elections in the Deccan were totally managed by north India. Nobody in the state was trusted. Mediocre leaders from Uttar Pradesh were sent to travel *incognito* in both the states to assess the "popularity" of aspirants for Congress tickets".[7] Even after the opposition made an issue of lack of respect for the party's own chief ministers by the Congress(I) high command, there was no concern for the sentiments of the common people. The prime minister never reassured the people of the two states that if her party emerged victorious, she would not impose her own choice as chief ministers. The central leadership of the Congress party seemed to forget that democracy cannot be remote controlled.

If the wounds to the regional pride were all too evident in Andhra Pradesh, they were also present at the subterranean level in Karnataka. The mishandling of Kannada language agitation and the farmers' agitation by the Congress(I) was felt an affront to the feelings of Kannadigas.

The peasantry is essentially tradition-bound and its perceptions are tied to things immediate to its existence. Local patriotism is characteristic of peasant attitudes. Peasants have been the backbone of linguistic agitations in our country. Since July 1980, Karnataka had witnessed one of the most militant peasant agitations in the country. The Congress(I) government handled the agitation by using force against the farmers. Police firings took place 139 times in Karnataka between July 1980 and December 1982, claiming over one hundred lives, mostly of the farmers.[8]

Language is the most important means of solidarity for the people to unite and on this issue also the Congress(I) government in Karnataka failed. People had a feeling that the chief minister Gundu Rao was basically a lover of Sanskrit and that he did not want Kannada to get primacy. It was said that he had packed the Gokak Committee that examined the question of state language with Sanskrit men. But they became fearful of public wrath, so they gave a report in favour of Kannada as the state language. That was too much for Gundu Rao to swallow.[9]

The issues raised by the farmers' agitation and the movement for the Kannada language touched the sensibilities of Kannadigas. While these issues were side-tracked by the Congress(I) in the name of national unity, people were searching for an instrument which could assuage their wounded self-respect. Kannada Kranti Ranga, a regional political party, served to focus the issues. When Kranti Ranga threw its weight behind Janata Party which had local leaders of distinction and stature at its helm (Janata at this time was nowhere in power and it had only a weak presence in Delhi) it became an efficient instrument to attract the support of the people.

Devaraj Urs, the founder of Kannada Kranti Ranga became a symbol of the Kannadiga aspirations. In 1979, when Devaraj Urs parted company with Indira Gandhi, it was not on any local issue but on national issues. The significance of Urs's departure from the Congress party for the common man in the local idiom was that their *Indramma* (Indira Gandhi) was alienated. The common man could not grasp the significance of the national issues on which Urs had parted company from *Indramma*. In reality, Indira Gandhi symbolised for the common man his local aspirations while Urs was seen as a more distant leader. Sympathy for her was evident in the 1980 Lok Sabha elections when all but one of the Congress(I) candidates had won but none of Urs's nominees was returned. But the common man's sympathy for *Indramma* took a dramatic twist when the people experienced the ignominy of rule by a ministry of defectors. The people's real problems were ignored under the pretext of resolving the national issues. As M.N. Srinivas has observed, Urs's sudden death in June 1982 produced a wave of sympathy for the dead hero, spotlighting his virtues and achievements: "Urs in death became more powerful than Urs alive" because, according to Srinivas, Urs's policy was essentially pragmatic and *specific* to Karnataka—"a radicalism that was *home-grown*"[10] (emphasis mine). In the same vein, he renamed Mysore as Karnataka on November 1, 1973 fulfilling the long cherished aspirations of the Kannadiga people. It is significant to note that Urs's radicalism did not involve even Mahatma Gandhi. Ambedkar, E.V.R. Naicker and Lohia were its heroes. Thus the image of the late Devaraj Urs as a symbol of modern Karnataka paid rich dividends when Janata-Kranti Ranga leaders successfully focussed people's attention on him and his ideals.

It may be noted here that after the 1983 elections, when the newly-elected governments in Andhra Pradesh and Karnataka came into power, they were very sensitive to the question of people's regional identity. The Janata government in Karnataka was quick in implementing the Kannada language policy. Teaching of Kannada in schools was made compulsory and it became the administrative language at all levels. In Andhra Pradesh, N.T. Rama Rao wanted to rename the state 'Telugu Nadu'. It is said that he did not like the word "Pradesh" because it had a Hindi ring about it.[11] He believed that renaming the state in his way would fully reflect the aspirations of all Telugus.

II

The crucial question is: What are the implications of the

awakening of the regional aspirations for India's federal polity? Will India disintegrate? The Congress leaders may see signs of danger to India's unity and integrity in this development. But a closer look at the issue provides us a different perspective.

As soon as he assumed power, N.T. Rama Rao made it clear that Telugu Desam was not a separatist party. While seeking more autonomy for the state, he stated categorically: "we stand for national unity and integration. We owe allegiance to the centre and wish to strengthen it so that it could fulfil its responsibilities".[12] Ramakrishna Hegde, the chief minister of Karnataka has said repeatedly that he did not want to confront the centre. On the other hand, several positive developments have taken place.

For instance, when water supply became an acute problem for the drying crops of Tanjore area in Tamil Nadu, the new Janata government in Karnataka released the necessary water from its Cauvery reserves without delay or intervention by the centre. Such a sharing of resources and coming to the help of neighbours in distress is a new idiom in Indian politics after the primordial loyalties have become dominant. No less a significant development are the reviews of centre—state relations. This was a critical subject for a long time. The decision to set up a council of chief ministers was a big step forward. It would help to carry out a thorough review of centre-state relations in order to strengthen "co-operative federalism" upon the basis of the experience of the past 35 years. Fiscal and administrative relations are the central issues. It is a plea for greater decentralisation. The chief ministers of Andhra Pradesh, Tamil Nadu and Pondicherry who met in Bangalore in March 1983 agreed that the existing Zonal Councils as well as the National Development Council were agencies of the central government and did not provide adequate opportunities for the states to express their points of view. The issues between the states could mostly be settled by themselves without running to the centre every time. The new initiative also provides an opportunity to review the status and powers of the governors. The functioning of governors of the states has come for close scrutiny in view of the events in the states. Girilal Jain wrote in *Times of India*: "She [Indira Gandhi] had managed to dispose of them [the SVD governments] by 1969 when she took on the 'Syndicate'. She used the centre-appointed governors in the states also to attain her objective."[13] The Janata government in Karnataka has raised this issue, hoping to focus the nation's attention on this neglected but crucial question that affects the Indian federal structure.[14]

The Indian people's affinity for and attachment to their mother tongue and all the ramifications arising therefrom cannot be over-emphasised. Linguistic identity evokes passions and emphasises the whole gamut of their cultural identity. When such an affinity is transformed into a community's collective consciousness, it becomes a powerful political force. This element in the psyche of old societies has convinced students of new states like Clifford Geertz to argue that primordial divisions are politically pathological and disintegrative in their consequences. Geertz writes: "Economic or class or intellectual disaffection threatens revolution, but disaffection based on race, language or culture threatens partition, irredentism, or merger, a redrawing of the very limits of the state, a new definition of its domain . . . Primordial discontent strives more deeply and is satisfied less easily."[15] Geertz argues that there is always the possibility of a direct conflict between primordial and civil sentiments.

India has been independent for thirty seven years. All segments of this nation avow that they are Indians, thus exposing the fallacy of Geertz's scepticism. On the other hand, the recognition and assertion of people's cultural identity and language have resulted in the political and economic striving for progress. This has unleashed their energies for social awareness and to a certain extent even "militant" group consciousness. In India, linguistic identity has been used to get a larger share of the nation's resources. Studies of demands based on language identity show that, under certain conditions, it helps to "strengthen the fabric of a new nation and its structure of authority and participation".[16] Demands based on language or ethnicity are not necessarily divisive or disintegrative. Das Gupta concludes that, if disintegrative consequences arise, the likelihood is that they were "determined by a variety of systemic and processual variables of politics causally unrelated to either ethnicity or primordiality". Therefore, "The labels of language or ethnicity do not necessarily invest any particularly divisive or disintegrative property on demands".[17] What stands disproved is that India will splinter into totalitarian small nationalities just because there are so many linguistically differentiated peoples, all of whom are so deeply self-aware.[18] Our experience has been that, independent of the intense primordial sentiments, there has been an overweening attachment to the central value system, in our case, the value of a united India. Evidently, each of these sentiments gets expression on various occasions such as elections for the state and the nation respectively.

Fears have now given way to confidence. The circumstances permit optimism and allow us to encourage the positive developments of people's identities, whether these are linguistic, cultural or religious. That will help in the growth of a vibrant society in the subcontinent. Excessive centralisation weakens people's sense of responsibility for public affairs and encourage the growth of negative aspects of primordial loyalties, e.g., communalism, sectarianism, etc. Balanced decentralisation and appropriate recognition of the regional initiative will promote a healthy federalism. Those who cry wolf at the slightest assertion of people's primordial identities are unwilling to face squarely the difficult problems that confront the people in their local situation.

III

Our main argument is that primordial linguistic identity provides an ideal setting for developing self-awareness and strengthening political consciousness. It also calls into question the veracity of the often repeated statement that Indira Gandhi's charisma is on the decline and that is why south India has voted against the Congress party. Charisma is a sociological term that has often been misused. Charisma, which in Greek means 'divine grace' was used by Ernst Troeltsch and then by Max Weber to designate the ability to lead and inspire the people by sheer force of personality and conviction but without the aid of material incentives or coercion.[19] A charismatic personality has no organised 'machine' at his disposal, his power has not been obtained through institutionalised procedure. By persuasion he attracts people to his message and secures their obedience. Gandhiji, before he acquired the backing of the party machine and Lenin, before his return to Russia, were charismatic leaders. "The opposite of a charismatic leader is a tyrant who rules through naked force and the fear which he inspires, or a ruler who is obeyed regardless of his personal capabilities and solely by virtue of the office which he holds".[20] A leader is charismatic so long as the number of followers remain small and it is the beginning of a movement. The term "charisma" becomes superfluous and confusing if it is used indiscriminately. Nonetheless, we cannot deny a charismatic aspect in some successful political leaders, whose faith and self-confidence prove infectious.

Charisma is also people's subjective perception of a person within their own sense of helplessness or in a situation where they believe that only a person endowed with extraordinary powers can help them to achieve certain goals, especially by transcending the accepted values and rules. As the people gain power and the ability to shape their own destiny, the need for or indispensability of the charismatic leaders disappears. We may argue, therefore, that when the people of Andhra Pradesh and Karnataka reached for their selfhood, they realised that they are the makers of their own future and it is absurd merely to ascribe the development to charismatic leaders endowed with supernatural powers.

CONCLUSION

It is significant that people of Andhra Pradesh and Karnataka expressed quite clearly that their demand for self identity through the symbols of primordial loyalties did not jeopardise their loyalty to the nation. In the present stage of the developments of our society, demands based on the primordiality of language, culture or religion, if stretched too far to the extent of parochialism, would be self-defeating. Regional chauvinism can whip up arrogance but in the face of increasing mobility of the people, the operation of national economic forces, communication networks and media influence and the widening network of persons (academics, writers, artists, professionals) who believe in a common humanity, it would be counter-productive. Demands for cultural strait-jackets bordering on fanaticism do great disservice to the cause they apparently want to serve. The limit to primordial fanaticism is evident from the history of Dravida Kazhagam in Tamil Nadu and Shiv Sena in Bombay.

Our concern in this paper is merely to delineate an important variable that affected the 1983 Andhra Pradesh and Karnataka elections and to analyse its implication for the Indian polity. This approach is not used in any value preferential way. In future it may be possible that people would participate in elections and raise their demands from a class perspective. Nonetheless the importance of peoples basic identity will remain an important sociological category and its heuristic significance to understand people's behaviour cannot be overestimated.

Notes and References

1. Edward Shils, Primordial, personal sacred and civil ties, *British Journal of Sociology*, Vol. 8, 1957, p. 133.
2. Selig S. Harrison, *India: The Most Dangerous Decades*, Oxford University Press, 1960, p. 1. "India stands the risk of being split up into a number of totalitarian small nationalities." (Suniti Kumar Chatterji, "Minority Report", Report of the Official Language Commission, Government of India Press, Delhi, 1957, p. 313).

   "The future is in the hands of the gods, but as far as I can judge, the centrifugal forces will ultimately prevail, and . . . the nation may be compelled to go through a period of political anarchy and face the risk of fascism, which is Nature's way out of disorder and misrule". (C. Rajagopalachari, *Our Democracy*, B.G. Paul & Co., Madras, 1957, p. 17).

   Then Harrison's remark was "When, in 1957, anxieties so often expressed in private could be committed to print, India had passed almost unnoticed from a remarkable Decade of Confidence into the first years of a struggle for simple national survival. Hope and strength were at bay. Frustration and defeat had taken the initiative".
3. *Ibid.*, p. 16.
4. Edward Shils, *op. cit.*, p. 133.
5. *Ibid.*, p. 130.

6. I have greatly benefited from a discussion with Prof. Surinder Suri, the noted political scientist on this aspect. Suri emphasises that this kind of regional solidarity helps to promote the development process because the energies of the peoples are not wasted on sectarian issues or other divisive considerations.
7. *The Week*, January 16-22, 1983, p. 7.
8. *The Other Side*, February 1983, p. 5.
9. *The Week*, January 2-8, 1983, p. 23.
10. M.N. Srinivas, Emerging indigenous radicalism, *Indian Express*, March 10, 1983.
11. *Deccan Herald*, January 10, 1983.
12. *Deccan Herald*, January 10, 1982.
13. *Times of India*, January 12, 1983.
14. The White Paper on *The Office of the Governor*, *Constitutional Position and Political Perversion* by the Government of Karnataka (1983), is a well-researched document for students of federalism.
15. Clifford Geertz, The integrative revolution, primordial sentiments and civil politics in the new states in his edited volume, *Old Societies and New States*, Glencoe, The Free Press, 1963, p. 111.
16. Jyotirindra Das Gupta, Ethnicity, language demands, and national development in India, in Nathan Glazer and Daniel P. Moynihan (eds.), *Ethnicity Theory and Experience*, Cambridge, Harvard University Press, 1978, p. 487.
17. *Ibid.*, p. 488.
18. Selig S. Harrison, *op. cit.*, p. 4.
19. S.L. Andreski in *A Dictionary of Sociology* edited by G. Duncan Mitchell, London, Routledge & Kegan Paul, 1977, p. 29.
20. *Ibid.*, p. 29.

Subject Index

Name Index

CHRISTIAN INSTITUTE FOR THE STUDY OF REGION AND SOCIETY

Studies on **Indian Democracy, Political Parties and Political Process.**

1. P.D. Devanandan, M.M. Thomas (eds.), *India's Quest for Democracy* (1955).
2. P.D. Devanandan, M.M. Thomas (eds.), *Cultural Foundations of Indian Democracy* (1955).
3. Herbert Jai Singh, Mark Sunder Rao (eds.) *Indian Politics after Nehru*, (1956).
4. J.R. Chandran, M.M. Thomas (eds.), *Political Outlook in India Today* (1956).
5. P.D. Devanandan, M.M. Thomas (eds.), *Problems of Indian Democracy* (1962).
6. Saral K. Chatterji (ed.), *The Coalition Government* (1974).
7. Saral K. Chatterji (ed.), *Political Prospects in India* (1971).
8. Saral K. Chatterji (ed.), *The Meaning of the Indian Experience: The Emergency* (1978).
9. "Indian Politics in the 1980s" (a study of the 1980 Parliamentary elections), *Religion and Society*, Vol. XXIX, No. 3, September 1982.